RAMBLING A....
FROM 'THE SMOKE'

The story of the ramblers' excursions
by train and coach from London
(1932 to 2004)
by
Colin Saunders
from an idea by
David Horwill

**With reminiscences from organisers,
leaders, rearguards and excursionists.**

**This book is dedicated to the memory of those
who made the ramblers' excursions possible and are
no longer with us, be they organisers, leaders or
rearguards; and to the excursionists, without whom
there would have been nobody to organise and lead.**

FOOTLINE PRESS

ISBN 978 0 9929434 0 0

Published by Footline Press Limited
35 Gerrards Close, Oakwood, London, N14 4RH, UK
Email: colin.saund@btconnect.com

Printed by Azimuth Print Ltd, Bowling Hill Business Park, Chipping Sodbury, Bristol, BS37 6JL

CONTENTS

PART 1 : THE RAMBLERS' EXCURSIONS STORY

There are also two appendices, which are only available online from the website *www.ramblingawayfromthesmoke.org.uk*.

Appendix A is a record all known excursions.
Appendix B lists the Commandos' footpath clearances.

ACKNOWLEDGEMENTS

Special thanks must be given to all those who organised the ramble excursions, without whom there would be no story to write – especially those who took on this task in the early years and carried the baton for so long, but are sadly no longer with us, in particular Hugh E. Page ('Pago'), John Grinsell, Len King, George Platt and Geoffrey Stevenson.

It is fitting that the social phenomenon of the ramblers' excursions from London, which lasted 72 years from 1932 to 2004, was closely linked to the lifespans of their most illustrious organisers. Although Hugh E. Page's life was ended prematurely by a road accident in 1958, the others died of natural causes: John Grinsell in 1986, George Platt in 1998 and Len King in 1999. Geoffrey Stevenson soldiered on, organising his own excursions for a few years after the demise, until he too was taken from us in 2010. Many others made substantial contributions, but this book should be considered as a lasting tribute to those five great men of the rambling world.

David Sharp, guidebook author and a Vice President of The Ramblers, compiled a feature on these excursions for *South Eastern Rambler* in July 1999. Some of his wry observations therein are too good to miss and have been reproduced where appropriate, with his permission.

The author is especially indebted to David Horwill, whose idea it was to write this story, and to the steering group who helped and advised him, consisting of David, his wife Brenda (Allen) Horwill, Graham Butler and Roger Kemp.

Many other people and organisations have contributed to or helped with this story. With apologies to anyone omitted, they include:

Kate Ashbrook, BBC Audience Services, Frank Barker, Angela (Ferrari) Bellwood, Brian Bellwood, Tom Berry, Rosie Binnie, Kathy (Stevenson) Brightwell, British Pathé, Joan Brown, Golfo Chrysanthopoulou, Graham Collett, Ted Cossor, Hugh Davies of the Railway Enthusiasts Club, Les Douglas, David and Sheila Dowsett, Frank Dring, Eric Ede, Richard Farrant, Paul Frances, Cyril Freeman, Bob Goodman, Jill Green, David Griffin, Chris Hall, Bridget Harper, Mike Herniman, Colin 'Inky' Hills, Pat Hills, Dick Hutchins, Madeline Hutchins, Richard Kendall, Chris Kew, Annette King, Michael Kohn, Diana (Hack) Lucas, John McGahern, The

Mail on Sunday, Alex Masson, Robert Maynard, Ian Mitchell, the National Railway Museum Search Engine, Ros Pool, Bill Ramsey, Brian Reader, Gill Reader, Arthur and Sheila Reed, Carl Roe, Ken Royce, Rosalie Saunders, Christopher Rule, Science & Society Picture Library, Celia (Grinsell) Short, Alan Smith, John Stebbings, Geoffrey Stevenson, Homer Sykes, Gary Thornton and his Six Bells Junction website, Geoffrey Waters, Pat Williamson and David Wright, plus members of the Connoisseur Rambling Club, Morley Ramblers, the Polytechnic Rambling Club, the Vanguards Rambling Club and the West London Ramblers, and all the rambling folk who have contributed to or are mentioned in various reminiscences. Details about S.P.B. Mais have been verified by reference to his biography, *An Unrepentant Englishman*, by Maisie Robson (The King's England Press, 2005).

S.P.B. Mais is surrounded by admiring fans on the occasion of 'Hiker's Mystery Express No.1' on 25 March 1932. [British Pathé]

FOREWORD

By Kate Ashbrook, General Secretary of the Open Spaces Society and President of The Ramblers.

There is much written today about the benefits of walking to the economy, how people spend when they go out walking, whether it's for the day or a longer break. This book tells of the time when the rail operators recognised and cashed in on the walkers' economy, and co-operated in running excursions, enabling ramblers to travel out on one line and back on another without having to buy expensive single tickets. There were even relief trains laid on in case too many people came!

The ups and downs in excursion history are recorded here: the Beeching axe which took 'at least 57 stations in good rambling country', the further blow in 1975 when Southern Region stopped the special trains for ramblers – and the weekend engineering works that allowed sufficient notice to organise an alternative excursion in the 1970s but not in the 1980s.

The book is important for many reasons. It is a valuable social history containing anecdotes and memories which would not otherwise have been recorded. The larger-than-life organisers, leaders and rearguards (as backmarkers were known), are recalled with affection and honesty, warts and all. I love the story of the leader who didn't want to fork out for a collection on behalf of the Ramblers, climbed up onto the luggage rack and pretended to be a suitcase. The book is crammed with recollections, many associated with pubs, such as the raucous return after a drink in the Fullers Arms (now the Berwick Inn) by Berwick station, near Lewes, which opened early to allow the ramblers to drink before the return train – and drink they did!

We don't do enough recording, and in this digital era the worry is that we shall do even less. Colin Saunders has done a great service and is an example to us all.

Things to draw to your attention

- The author has tried to contact as many former organisers, leaders and excursionists as possible, but inevitably some will have escaped the net. If, after reading this document, you feel that something noteworthy has been omitted, or if you believe any statements to be incorrect, please contact the publisher.

- It is intended that there will be a blog dedicated to this history, where relevant additional items and information may be published, with your permission – though they may have to be edited. For more information please refer to the website: *www.ramblingawayfromthesmoke.org.uk*

- In due course, a new edition of this book may be published, so that any relevant corrections and additions can be incorporated.

- This book only concerns itself with rambler's excursions from London, but it is recognised that they have taken place in many other parts of the country, especially from major industrial centres further north such as Manchester, Leeds, Liverpool, Newcastle, Nottingham and Sheffield.

- Frequent reference is made to the 'Ramblers' Association' or 'the RA'. It was established in 1931 as the National Council of Ramblers' Federations, then in 1935 the name was changed to the Ramblers' Association. In 2009 it was rebranded simply as The Ramblers. However, throughout the period when these excursions operated, it was known by its previous names, so they are used in this book. For further information about The Ramblers, visit their website *www.ramblers.org.uk*.

- An e-book version of this story will be made available in due course from the website *www.ramblingawayfromthesmoke.org.uk*.

SUMMER HAZE

In the depths of a long winter's evening,
Our thoughts turn to hot summer days;
Those are now rapidly coming
To spots that delight and amaze.
To Elgar's beloved green country
At the foot of the great Malvern Hills
For a pomp and a circumstance march
To drive away all winter's ills.
Beyond Ashford to Sandling and Folkestone,
Perhaps to that vast Tunnel mouth;
We'll promise you not to walk through it
But plan to go round, north or south.
Seawards, by ferry to Ryde,
And shanks pony to Shanklin, maybe;
Then a tube through the rich countryside
For fine sights of the Solent and sea.
Seven Sisters, all in white, stand proud
From the cliffs above Cuckmere to view,
Whilst above, skies without e'en a cloud
Give us walking of varying hue.
So join us for one of our rambles;
Destinations inside, old and new,
These places and more are on offer,
For the many, and not for the few.
(David Horwill, London Rambler, May 2000)

JOG ON

Jog on, jog on, the footpath way,
And merrily hent* the stile-a.
A merry heart goes all the day.
Your sad tires in a mile-a.
(Autolycus, The Winter's Tale)

* Hent is an old English word meaning 'seize'.

SOME PERSONAL THOUGHTS

From David Horwill

Having moved from the great rambling county of Gloucestershire to live in London, I soon discovered that there were strolls being led nearly every Saturday afternoon, mainly by Les Douglas. But I realised I wanted something more challenging, and spotting a leaflet for some train rambles at a main line station, what better way to combine two interests, railways and rambling, so I went on my first train ramble to Shawford on 20 August 1989. It was a little while before I ventured out again, this time to Brookwood and met Brenda Allen who introduced me to Bridget Harper. From then on I began to act as a rearguard for Bridget, until such time as things started to get somewhat serious between Brenda and me, leading to our teaming up for both marriage and rambling. The rest, as they say, is history.

After the train rambles came to an end in December 2004, a discussion took place at the following Inner London Area AGM about the train and coach rambles. There was agreement that their story should not be lost and I volunteered to attempt writing it all up. But the first thing was to collect some data in the form of itineraries, leaflets, promotional material etc, and then to obtain background details, which resulted in a long interview with Geoffrey Stevenson shortly before he died. Of those from the early days, he was by far the most knowledgeable person around. So began the marathon task, whose mantle has been kindly taken up by Colin Saunders, to great effect.

From Brenda Horwill

Family history led me to The Ramblers! I am interested in the subject and my ancestors came from around Rowland's Castle. For a couple of years I had seen Ramblers' leaflets at London mainline stations but then found one that included a ramble starting from Rowland's Castle station! However, the leaflet advertised rambles nearly every Sunday, so my first experience of a led walk was on 7

August 1988 on a ramble from Lenham in Kent. It was so exciting walking in the countryside that I immediately joined The Ramblers.

My idea was to ramble once a month, but found that ramblers were so friendly that it was very soon fortnightly, then weekly. My third ramble was from Rowland's Castle and it was great walking in the footsteps of my ancestors!

On 11 June 1989 I rearguarded on a Family Rambling Day walk and three months later led my first ramble. However, my second was a little problematical with 53 in the party! Due to various circumstances 27 got mislaid, but I learnt lessons and it didn't stop me leading.

Rambling has proved brilliant for making new friends. On 17 December 1989, during a Brookwood ramble, I met David Horwill and 14 months later we were married! We continue to lead rambles together.

David and Brenda Horwill

From Colin Saunders

I have spent and enjoyed most of my adult leisure time as a rambler, and this is due to the ramblers' excursions from London. At a particularly low time after breaking up with a girl friend, a colleague at work, Richard Farrant, suggested that I should join him on the excursion on 9 April 1967 to Amberley and Arundel. I did just that, fell in with those unruly reprobates, the Vanguards, and had a whale of a time. I became a regular ramblers' excursionist, soon a rearguard, then a leader. I almost forgot the girl friend!

Now, nearly half a century later, I have made a tenuous living out of walking by organising holidays and events, managing a trail and writing books. I owe so much to the ramblers' excursions and was delighted when David Horwill asked if I would write up their history, which I have been happy to do on a purely voluntary basis.

Thank you for reading this, I hope it will bring back many happy memories, as it has done for me.

See page 94 for an image of the author – if you must!

"**The vast throngs of ramblers** no longer tumble out of special trains, filling the forecourt while leaders try to sort out who is going with whom, and organisers phone tea places with astronomical numbers, and clubs wonder how long they will have to wait for the second half of their party to arrive on the relief train. The great ramble excursions from London are just a page of ramblers' history – but too important to be forgotten. In their time, they must have taken some half a million people out of London, introducing two whole generations to countrygoing."

David Sharp, South Eastern Rambler, July 1999.

For many, those were life-changing journeys and Sundays would never be the same again.

WHAT'S IN A NAME?

Whilst the Inuit are said to have many words for snow, it seems that English-speakers have as many, if not more, for walking: ambling, dawdling, footing, gadding, gallivanting, hiking, hoofing, pacing, perambulating, plodding, pootling, sauntering, shuffling, staggering, stepping, striding, strolling, strutting, stomping, stumping, toddling, tottering, traipesing, tramping, treading, trekking, waddling, wandering.....and rambling. And many more in regional dialects. They all mean, to some degree or other, putting one foot in front of the other, over and over again.

The journeys that form the subject of this story were always known as *ramblers' excursions*, so (with apologies to those who prefer anything else) 'ramble' and its derivatives is the term we shall be using.

The headboard says 'Conducted Rambles Jubilee Excursion' – probably the Silver Jubilee excursion to Dorchester South, Upwey and Weymouth on 21 April 1957. George Platt, to the right of the engine, is about to be engulfed in steam.

1 : INTRODUCTION

This is the story of a 20th century social phenomenon, the ramblers' excursions from London. It grew from a desire by people living in the capital ('The Smoke') to get away from it on at least one day a week and explore the surrounding countryside.

Sadly, few of today's younger generation of ramblers will be aware of those excursions, which lasted from 1932 to 2004, and the important part they played in the growth of walking as a leisure activity. The early excursion programmes used special trains, but later ones also went by coach. To their devotees they were known simply as 'train rambles' and 'coach rambles'.

The author hopes that this book will set all this down for the benefit of social historians of the present and future, as well as bring back happy memories for those who participated.

The crying shame is that we have been unable to trace the most comprehensive archives about the excursions that we know of, held by the late Geoffrey Stevenson and John Grinsell. From various sources, we have been able to recreate an almost complete list of the dates and destinations of all the excursions in Appendix A (available from the website *www.ramblingawayfromthesmoke.org.uk*) but sadly details of many of the early excursions are missing. At the time of writing, this appendix ran to 160 pages so you are strongly advised not to print it out! We suggest that, if possible, you just refer to it on screen when necessary.

All the early organisers and many of the leaders have now passed away, so it has not been possible for us to ask them to check and verify the text, or to add their experiences. Fortunately, before Geoffrey Stevenson died in 2010, David Horwill was able to interview him and get much information. It has to be said that, in some cases, the information gleaned from various sources is conflicting and confusing – memory can sometimes play havoc with the facts – but we have tried to present the story as fairly and accurately as possible. No doubt readers will get in touch if they think that any details are wrong or anything of significance has been omitted.

It is intended that the website *www.ramblingawayfromthesmoke.org.uk* will include a link to a blog, on which further experiences and information can be added. If enough extra material comes to light, it may lead to a second edition.

Hopefully, those who read this document will ransack their brains and diaries, their cupboards and attics, and contact the publisher if they come across any information that will add to the story, be it bare facts or reminiscences about things that happened on an excursion. Please don't be shy: your contribution can be 'ghost-written' if you would rather not do it yourself, and can be anonymous if you prefer.

The book will also be lodged with the British Library and the other Legal Deposit Libraries in the hope that it will provide useful material for those who wish to research this small corner of social history.

What is rambling?

Ignoring its other meanings, for our purpose 'rambling' is defined by the Oxford English Dictionary as 'the activity of walking in the countryside for pleasure', and its first known use in this sense was in the 17th century. Detractors may scoff, but you can now proudly inform them that it derives from an old Dutch word, *rammelen*, meaning 'to wander about on heat'! This may seem curious, suggesting an element of sexual arousal, but when the 17th century poet and rake, John Wilmot, 2nd Earl of Rochester (1647-1680) wrote *A Ramble in St James's Park*, it was clear that his use of the expression made this activity more akin to modern-day kerb-crawling!

Walking is one of the most basic actions that humans can engage in. Over hundreds of millennia, *homo sapiens* evolved to walk, and whereas most mammals can spend little time raised on their hind feet, let alone make forward progress, the human frame lends itself to standing erect and placing one foot in front of the other without falling over, for hours on end.

In the beginning, walking or running were the only means of getting from place to place, and nomadic humans had to follow on foot their need for food and habitable land. Much later, horses were tamed and ridden, but in most communities this was only for the elite, who could afford to buy or borrow a horse, or ride in a stagecoach. Ordinary village folk gave a sardonic nod to their lack of equestrian transport by saying they would go on 'shanks pony' – on foot! (The reference being to the part of the leg between knee and ankle.) Normally, their only objectives were to go to church, market or place of work, or to buy food or visit the local hostelry. The longest journeys made by most, still on foot, were to visit kinsfolk who had married someone in the next village.

Walking was rarely done for its own sake, but wandering around the countryside inspired many writers and poets, among them Wordsworth, Coleridge and Dickens. Others ventured further afield for days or months on end, sleeping wherever they could find a bed or barn, and later writing about their travels. Though they probably didn't think of it as such, what they were doing was.....rambling!

What is an excursion?

The OED tells us that one of the meanings of 'excursion' is 'a short journey or trip, especially one taken as a leisure activity'. It comes from the Latin verb *excurrere*, meaning to run out, and its first known use in this sense was in the late 17th century.

It is perhaps those artistic folk that we must thank for opening up our vision of the wonderful world beyond the daily grind. So why shouldn't ordinary men and women enjoy such pleasures? Ah yes, but who had the time? If they had the time how could they get there? And if they could get there, what then?

To make matters worse, while poets had the time and inclination to wander lonely as a cloud praising daffodils, skylarks, mountains and anything else that took their fancy, from the late 18th century the

14

industrial revolution led to an increasing migration of working people to towns and cities, and estrangement from the countryside they loved. Walking was definitely not inspiring for those who had to live in grimy cities.

Working people knew how lovely the countryside was, yet were unable to reach it, and this contributed to their resentment, unhappiness, ill-health and poor performance at work. There was a real need to get out of the smoke-ridden atmosphere of the cities and to enjoy 'fresh air'. Reformers and the more enlightened employers and politicians came to realise that much of this misery could be resolved by creating parks in which to wander, and introducing weekend breaks and, later, holidays.

Meanwhile, in the early 19th century, along came trains, and a network of railway lines that by the 1850s had grown to cover much of Britain. And in 1841 along came a thoughtful Leicestershire cabinet-maker called Thomas Cook. He was sure that the social problems of the time were the result of alcohol, and one day had the bright idea of organising an excursion by train from Leicester to an important temperance meeting in Loughborough. On that first excursion, 500 people each paid a shilling (5p, equal to £7.25 in 2014) to ride on wooden seats in open carriages for twelve miles each way, but in time such journeys (in more comfortable rolling stock) would carry millions all over the country for all sorts of reasons including football matches, mystery tours, brewery visits (oh, how Thomas Cook would spin in his grave)....and rambling!

Finding the way

We owe so much to those ordinary village folk we encountered earlier. By plodding day after day from home to place of work to church to pub to shop and back over many centuries, and by visiting kinsfolk in the next village, they created paths that eventually became enshrined in law as rights of way. These paths linked up to form a dense network of routes in England and Wales that we can still ramble over, getting away from traffic to enjoy a real countryside experience. Add to these the vast areas of access land, where even

15

such as we can wander lonely as a cloud, and we have in our island what should be a ramblers' paradise – assuming, of course, that the highway authorities keep those paths in good order! And, unlike much of the globe, Britain is largely free of beasts that may inflict grievous wounds. A veritable rambler's paradise!

This is all very fine in theory, it's natural to want to explore, be it one's immediate surroundings or further afield. But when you get out there and actually have to decide which way to go, it can all seem so much harder than you imagined. Suppose you got lost, or benighted, or told to 'git orf moi larnd' by a furious farmer? No, far better to stay at home. But what if somebody else organised it all for you, and led the way, and found a fine old inn for lunch, and somewhere nice for tea and cake later? Better still, what if you could meet new friends or even find romance? The solution was at hand .....the Ramblers' Excursions!

What next?

There had been embryonic signs of organised rambling in the early 19th century: the snappily named Association for the Protection of Ancient Footpaths in the Vicinity of York was established in 1824, closely followed by the Manchester Association for the Preservation of Ancient Footpaths in 1826 – the knack of devising catchy acronyms had still to be mastered. London had to wait until 1865, when the Commons Preservation Society (now the Open Spaces Society) was set up to campaign for access to common land, not only in the capital but throughout the UK.

But walking for pleasure really took off later that century, for by then the railway network had virtually reached its peak and getting out into the countryside was easy. The opportunity had arrived to take a break from the drudgery of normal routine and experience a life of fresh air and exercise – on Sundays at least as most people had to work on Saturdays then.

London is surrounded by vast swathes of ideal walking country, even more so in those days, where you would not be too far from home and there were plenty of trains and buses to take you there and back.

The railway companies wanted to fill their trains at weekends and offered cheap day returns to seaside resorts and places such as Box Hill, where horse-drawn carts were laid on to transport passengers up to the viewpoint and tea-room, and where the more adventurous might apprehensively explore nearby woods, downs and fieldpaths.

A few enterprising individuals wrote about their rambling experiences, setting out specific route instructions for their readers to follow in booklets (some of which were published by the railway companies) or in newspapers and magazines. They included the self-styled and prolific 'Walker Miles' (Edmund Seyfang Taylor, 1853-1908), whose series of 'sixpenny fieldpath guides' was published in the late 19th and early 20th centuries. Indeed this style of rambling continues right through to the present day in one form or another.

The 'Search Engine' (archives) of the National Railway Museum in York holds copies of such guidebooks published in the early part of the 20th century. For example, one published c 1900 by the London Brighton & South Coast Railway of rambles in Sussex; another in 1915 by the London & South Western Railway entitled *Pleasant paths for ramblers*; another c 1925 by the London Midland & Scottish Railway of *Rambles round London in the delightful districts served by the LMS*, and a series published c 1930 by the London & North Eastern Railway of rambles in the counties they served by, variously, F.H. Headley, Bernard Reeves and someone known simply as 'Pathfinder'.

But of more significance for our story, some very popular guidebooks describing rambles in various parts of southern England were published from the early 1930s onwards by two other railway companies. They were written by two rambling superstars of their time: S.P.B. Mais (for the Southern Railway) and Hugh E. Page (for the Great Western) – of whom more later.

Yet most people were in awe of a countryside they did not know. Few could read or understand maps, or felt confident to explore unknown territory on their own. And many people wanted to be led, with someone else taking on the responsibility for deciding where to go. Organisation and leadership were needed.

To some extent this was provided by rambling clubs, which had started to appear: the earliest we know of in the London area were the Sunday Tramps in 1879 (no longer in existence but a history has been published), the Forest Ramblers in 1884 and the Regent Street Polytechnic Rambling Club in 1885 (both still going strong and believed to be the oldest extant rambling clubs in Britain). But at this time such clubs were regarded as somewhat exclusive and dominated by men, indeed most were for 'gentlemen' only.

And so it went on until the First World War, when so many men were lost and by which time the suffragette movement was in full swing. In 1915, the Highbury United Rambling Club avertised itself as 'open to either sex', and other clubs soon followed suit. In the late 1920s, the Northampton Polytechnic Rambling Club (actually based in London's Northampton Square and now known as City University London) organised ramble excursions by coach for its members – one even included a short hop by aeroplane to the Isle of Wight – and other clubs took up the idea, but these outings were for members only.

In 1932 the mass trespass on Kinder Scout created huge publicity and encouraged many more people to think about getting out into the countryside (though preferably without all that fuss and bother and ending up in jail), but they wanted to be organised and led. At that time, what is now known as The Ramblers* was in its infancy and in no position to organise excursions, so some enterprising individuals took matters into their own hands and set about creating.....the Ramblers' Excursions!

*Regional associations of rambling clubs started to emerge in the early 20th century. They included the so-called Federation of Rambling Clubs, founded by Walker Miles and others in 1905, though this was actually southern-based. Although similar federations of local rambling clubs were established soon afterwards in other areas, the national organisation was established in 1931 as the National Council of Ramblers' Federations, renamed the Ramblers' Association in 1935, and The Ramblers in 2009. Nowadays it provides a multitude of led walks for members every weekend and annual walking festivals for the general public).

2: THE TRAIN RAMBLES

The start

The origin of the special ramblers' excursions by train from London can be traced back to the Easter weekend of 25-28 March 1932. An item in *Railway Magazine* said:

The GWR organised two special 'Hikers' Mystery Expresses', the first of which set out from Paddington at 10.25 a.m on Good Friday to destinations unknown to the passengers, driver and guard until after the train had started. This mystery element seems to have caught the imagination of the public beyond all expectation, for an hour before the train was due to leave, Paddington station was overwhelmed with hikers, and two trains had to be run to accommodate the 1,500 who presented themselves. The 'Hikers' Mystery Express No.1', which consisted of twelve third-class corridor coaches, was drawn by a 4-6-0 locomotive No.4002, *Evening Star*. Special posters with the name of the train were displayed on the front of the smokebox and on the side of the tender. Smaller posters were also pasted on the coach windows.

As soon as the train had left Paddington a copy of *Rambles in the Chiltern Country*, containing detailed descriptions of twentyfive walks through delightful country served by the Great Western Railway, was presented to each passenger, together with a pamphlet revealing the fact that the train would make its first stop at Tilehurst and then proceed as far as Pangbourne. The return journey was timed for a departure from Pangbourne at 6.50 p.m and Tilehurst at 6.57 p.m, arriving back at Paddington at 7.45 p.m.

On the following Sunday the 'Hikers' Mystery Express No.2' left Paddington under similar conditions for Henley-on-Thames. The weather being bad, however, only 550 travelled on the train.

Note that this particular 'Evening Star' locomotive is not the one that has been preserved at the National Railway Museum in York. Also, before anyone comments, it should be noted that the pamphlet referred to above said Hiker's not Hikers', but the item was written in the knowledge that more than one hiker turned up! A copy of this pamphlet is held in the archives of the National Railway Museum, and an image of it is reproduced on the front cover of this book.

Note how the GWR managed to provide an extra train at short notice. It seems to have been the case in those days that there was a considerable amount of spare capacity of both rolling stock and staff, which would not be available now.

At this time public rights of way were not shown as such on maps – we had to wait until the National Parks and Access to the Countryside Act of 1949 for that. What were known as 'field paths' existed, but few people had the knowledge or confidence to use them, so the described routes on offer mostly followed what were then quiet roads and lanes. Imagine: hundreds of people from London descending from a wayside station and setting off along the local roads – the complete reverse of commuting – and all trying to follow their little guidebook. To quote David Sharp in *South Eastern Rambler*: "The day's biggest mystery was how everyone managed to get back to the train again!"

A statement in that pamphlet said "passengers desirous of making a Week-End Hike may return any day up to Tuesday March 29th inclusive upon additional payment of three shillings". Presumably it was expected that some people, not knowing the destination in advance, would be willing to take a chance on finding accommodation at short notice, or were prepared to sleep under a hedge!

On board these excursions were the aforementioned Messrs S.P.B. Mais and H.E. Page, both well known writers of walk books. (In those days it was considered improper to reveal one's forename to the public!) They were very keen walkers and were so impressed by the success of these experimental excursions that they persuaded both the Southern Railway and the London & North Eastern Railway (LNER) to lay on special excursions for ramblers.

It seems very likely that others on that Mystery Excursion included a Mr J.T. Grinsell and a Mr L.R. King of the Sussex Pathfinders Walking Club, who were to play major roles in the subsequent development of ramblers' excursions on the LNER and the London Midland & Scottish Railway (LMS), as well as those by coach. More of these gentlemen later. Others who are thought to have travelled that day include Bernard Broadway, Freddie Fear, Horace Huxley and Louise Holford, all of whom became regular leaders and rearguards on the excursions.

The 'Great Hiking Boom' was well under way, and the significance of this can be inferred from the inclusion, in a 2013 BBC series entitled *Heritage – the battle for Britain's past*, of a very brief clip from a black-and-white silent movie made on Hikers' Mystery Express No.1. A more extended version of this movie, entitled 'Hiking Up To Date', can be viewed on the British Pathé website *www.britishpathe.com* (search for 'hiking up to date'). It lasts about two minutes including a short advert at the start. The bespectacled gentleman with a trilby hat, pipe and walking stick, surrounded by a bevy of admiring ladies, is believed to be none other than the aforementioned Mr Mais, who was quite a celebrity at the time (see photograph on page 4).

In the years that followed, until the outbreak of the Second World War, London ramblers were spoilt for choice, with as many as three different excursions on offer on some dates. Details of many of them are shown in our Appendix A (see page 2).

South of the Thames

For Londoners most good walking country lies to the south, in the North and South Downs, the Weald and the south coast, so it was natural that the majority of excursions would head in that direction. This was reflected by the more frequent excursions provided by the Southern Railway and the higher attendances they achieved. Indeed, special trains for ramblers seem to have been a Southern phenomenon, as trips organised on other lines were apparently by scheduled service trains with reserved carriages for ramblers, sometimes involving a change en route.

The first excursion on Southern ran on Whit Sunday 15 May 1932 and was advertised thus:

Note the sly dig at GWR's mystery excursions! The return fare would have been around 3 shillings (15 pence, the equivalent of £7.35 in 2014), travelling in third class carriages*. On that first excursion, more than 500 passengers turned out in two trains and seven parties were offered, with distances between 10 and 19 miles.

* Railway companies operated a three-class system at that time and third class carriages were used until they were abolished in 1956, after which second class (later renamed standard class) carriages were used. Incidentally, the second class fares that were introduced then were based on those that were applied to the ramblers' excursions, which shows the high standing of these excursions during that period.

The idea became instantly popular and Southern produced a leaflet entitled 'Sunday Walks with Mr S.P.B. Mais' (the great man indeed accompanied some of the trips in their early years), using 'corridor special trains', with the programme being organised by Mr H.E. Page. Except during the Second World War and its aftermath, such leaflets containing details of forthcoming ramble excursions continued to be published for the next seven decades and became required reading for an army of Londoners.

In 1932 the Southern excursions ran on alternate Sundays in summer and monthly in winter out of Victoria, Charing Cross, Waterloo and occasionally London Bridge or Blackfriars. We have no details for 1933, but presumably they were still running fortnightly as Mr Page was by then also organising fortnightly trips for the LNER (see 'North of the Thames' below). By 1934 and 1935 they were operating weekly in summer and fortnightly in winter, and from 1936 they ran weekly throughout the year, except for the weekend before Christmas (traditionally left clear for shopping). Southern's excursions also operated on most bank holiday Mondays as well as Good Friday, and even on Boxing Day in some years.

An item in *Railways South East* in 1992 about the early days of ramble excursions by train stated that 54 such excursions had taken place in 1936 carrying a total of 27,609 ramblers – an average of 511 per trip. (Presumably this relates to excursions on the Southern Railway only.)

Soon average attendances had grown to 600-700 with as many as nine parties, and Southern Railway were sufficiently confident of the attendance to justify providing a relief train in case of need (as proved the case on many dates). Southern devised the slogan 'South for Scenery!' for these excursions.

It was stressed that the excursions were open to all, though there was gentle encouragement to join the newly-formed Ramblers' Association, and this remained the case throughout the existence of these excursions.

H.E. Page tried (and mostly succeeded with) some very imaginative ideas, including:

- *10-11 September 1932:* A 'Harvest Moon Ramble' to Hassocks, to see the sunrise from Ditchling Beacon, leaving Victoria just after midnight and returning the following morning. S.P.B. Mais was billed to deliver a short lecture at dawn.

- *5 November 1932:* A 'Moonlight Ramble' to Brighton, when ramblers carried a Chinese lantern up to the bonfire and fireworks on Devil's Dyke. This was followed by a dinner-dance in Brighton and a ramble in the South Downs next day. Such outings proved enormously popular and similar ones (without the dinner-dance) featured as 'Moonlight and Sunrise Rambles' in the summer of following years, leaving London around midnight and returning either early next morning or later to allow a full day's walk. Such journeys originally included a refreshment or buffet car on the train, but this practice was discontinued after 1935 – maybe they didn't pay.

- *27 December 1932:* A Christmas ramble to Witley and Haslemere, including a lantern procession around the Devil's Punchbowl after tea.

- *31 December 1932:* A New Year's Eve ramble to Hassocks including 'a surprise item'. This turned out to be a bonfire on the Devil's Dyke, followed by a New Year Dance at Sherry's in Brighton from 2.15 to 6 a.m. There was an optional all-day walk on New Year's Day with the Sussex Pathfinders Walking Club, and therefore probably led by J.T. Grinsell with L.R. King as his rearguard.

- *6 August 1934:* A 'no passport required' bank holiday day trip to Boulogne for *rambles* among the surrounding woods and cliffs, departed Victoria 8.44 a.m and returned there at 11.05 p.m using the Southern Railway 'turbine mail steamer' from Folkestone.

- An annual 'no passport' weekend excursion to France over the Whitsun bank holiday. The first of these in August 1935 left London on Saturday evening *and* went via Newhaven to Dieppe, where participants where deposited in the small hours for a sunrise walk among the cliffs and woods of Normandy. Dieppe was the destination again in 1936 and 1937, but in 1938 the journey was extended to Rouen, and in 1939 to Paris. David Sharp remarked in *South Eastern Rambler:* "What Parisiennes made of all these ramblers tramping the boulevards in search of cream teas is not recorded". The return trip was usually on Sunday afternoon, but some arrived back on bank holiday Monday morning with an option to walk from Newhaven across the South Downs to Lewes or Brighton and return by any train from there.

- Long-distance trips to Dartmoor (Okehampton, Bridestowe, Brentor, 16 May 1937) and South Devon (Axminster, Seaton, Honiton, 31 July 1938) that took advantage of long summer days to start the return journey around midnight and arrive back in

London at around 6.30 a.m. Alternatively, on payment of a small supplement, passengers could alight during the return journey to join the following day's scheduled excursion, which was arranged somewhere along the homeward route.

- A Saturday afternoon ramble and tea dance to Maidstone East on 31 October 1936 (repeated on 6 March 1937) – though this idea had already been introduced by J.T. Grinsell for an LMS excursion to Hemel Hempstead in April 1935. The train left Charing Cross at lunchtime, a cream tea and late refreshments were provided and the dance took place in 'a magnificent hall with sprung floor'. In case anyone was tempted to dance in their muddy walking boots, the programme advised that dancing shoes were essential! A moonlight ramble was offered to non-dancers before the train returned soon after 9 p.m.

One gets the impression that ramblers of that era had more stamina than now! There must have been a wonderful atmosphere on those trips – perhaps it's a shame that such offerings are not tried nowadays.

Dancing appeared to be a popular alternative activity for many ramblers, and H.E. Page organised some well attended 'Southern Region Ramblers' Reunion Dances' at central London venues on winter evenings between 1934 and 1939.

At some stage a badge was produced for the excursionists to wear, as a means of recognising their fellow travellers. At the instigation of George Platt (of whom more later), the badge was reproduced in 1963, as a limited edition of 250, and sold for 2s 6d (12½p).

A glance through Appendix A (see page 2) shows that many of the early destinations will be familiar to more recent excursionists, but now, post-war and post-Beeching, we can only drool at the choice on offer. It's also noticeable that many destinations could then be used that are now too built-up to be of interest to ramblers.

Contrary to popular perception, allowing for inflation the fares offered in the early days were much in line with those in force in the final season of the excursions in 2004. On Southern in the mid 1930s they ranged from 2s 0d to 10s 6d in old shillings and pence, the equivalent of £4.88 to £24.31 in 2004, while a ramblers' day-trip to Dieppe cost £1 2s 6d (£51.14 in 2004).

The journeys took longer than now, for example:
- Victoria to Uckfield was 1 hour 38 minutes (now 1h 19m)
- Waterloo to Godalming 1h 5m (45 minutes)
- Charing Cross to Paddock Wood 1h 7m (46 minutes)

But of course there was the convenience, on Southern at least, of having a special train going direct to and from the stations where the rambles would start or finish.

It should be noted that a leaflet published by Southern Railway in 1933 showed that J.T. Grinsell planned and led ramble excursions for them from Brighton and other Sussex coast towns on Mondays and Wednesdays in August and September of that year.

North of the Thames

Although we have almost no literature for the GWR, it is believed that at first they continued to run 'Ramblers' Specials' on the lines of their original 'Mystery Excursion', with ramblers being given copies of books by either S.P.B. Mais or H.E. Page and left to their own devices. The only other pre-war dates we have are 5 November 1933 to Maidenhead and Henley-on-Thames (its handbill included a plug for Page's book, *Rambles in the Chiltern Country*), and 13 April 1936 (Easter Monday) when the destination was Pangbourne. For the latter, several hundred tickets were quickly sold to fill the train and another had to be hired soon afterwards for those who were unable to enjoy the first trip. Like on the original mystery excursions, it seems that no leaders were provided, just a booklet of suggested walks in the area.

At this time there was very keen rivalry between the four great railway companies, and it was not long before the other two latched on. Information about their early excursions is patchy, but in 1933 the London & North Eastern Railway (LNER) published a leaflet of *Conducted Rambles in Bucks Essex Herts under the auspices of Mr Hugh*

E. Page (who seemed to have a monopoly of organising at this time). They operated fortnightly from mid April to mid September, plus one in October, out of Marylebone, Kings Cross or Liverpool Street. The leaflet stated that the rambles would be led 'mainly by experienced members of London Rambling Clubs' and that 'everything possible will be done to carry them through without a hitch'. Lunch boxes were on sale on the platform at the London termini for a shilling (5p, which equates to £2.50 in 2014).

Another LNER leaflet from 1933 shows H.E. Page organising conducted rambles from North Weald, Blake Hall and Ongar on 27 August of that year; it offered a choice of six rambles ranging in distance from 10 to 15 miles and led by Messrs D.C.M. Gardner, G.W. Wallington, N.A. Burchill (of whom more later), H. Tanner, A.T. Nelson and G. Quantrill. Strangely, travel arrangements and start time are not indicated.

It may be surmised that, by now, H.E. Page was finding it difficult to organise all the ramble excursions out of London, and in 1933 J.T. Grinsell took over as organiser for the London Midland & Scottish Railway (LMS), operating out of Euston, St Pancras or occasionally Fenchurch Street, and the following year did the same for the LNER. But as Grinsell couldn't be in two places at once, the LNER and LMS dates alternated between the two systems. Page now confined himself to weekly excursions for Southern, but these two gentlemen were building rival empires in the rambling world and going head-to-head with competing excursions on the same dates on most weekends in the 1930s.

Like Southern, LMS were willing to include some more adventurous offerings including occasional dawn rambles and tea-dances. They had the advantage of serving more adventurous terrain and on bank holiday weekends provided long-distance excursions to the moorlands of the Peak District, Snowdonia, the Yorkshire Moors and the Lake District.

One such jaunt to Windermere included a sunrise ascent of Helvellyn, walking down to Keswick for breakfast, then a leisurely ramble in Borrowdale and return to London on Sunday evening.

Another deposited ramblers back in London at 4.50 a.m on the Monday (not a bank holiday), giving time to go home and change before going straight back out again to work! As David Sharp observed in *South Eastern Rambler*: "One imagines some bleary-eyed ramblers struggling to work on Monday morning!" As with Southern, an early experiment to include a restaurant car on these long-distance trains was apparently not very successful, and they were soon dropped. Ramblers have a (possibly deserved) reputation for being tight-fisted, and it was likely that most of them took sandwiches and a Thermos flask.

Following the introduction of half-day Saturday working for most employees earlier in the 20th century, between 1935 and 1939 J.T. Grinsell organised some very popular Saturday afternoon excursions for the LMS (and later LNER) to places not far from London, including a stop for afternoon tea. It was sometimes possible to go on the Saturday afternoon trip, returning to London around 10 p.m, then join the overnight train soon after midnight for an excursion to the moors. Those pre-war ramblers were certainly keen!

There's an apparent mystery in Summer 1936 when two LMS excursions ran simultaneously, but this can be explained. From 1936 J.T. Grinsell was assisted by L.R. King so could have covered both between them. They were just as busy as H.E. Page down at Southern, and on some weekends provided three ramblers' excursions: Saturday afternoon, overnight Saturday-Sunday and Sunday daytime.

Not included in our list of excursions are some inclusive rambling holidays and weekend breaks that J.T. Grinsell organised in the 1930s for LMS on several occasions at Easter and Christmas, to such places as the Lake District, Rutland and Lincolnshire. (He continued to do this for Christmas after the war, nominally for Grinsell's Rambling Club but all his excursionist friends were welcome, to places such as Bristol and Norwich.)

It is noticeable that the LMS excursions operated to some destinations several times each year, and this is probably due to the relatively restricted choice compared with those available on Southern.

See page 98 for a graphic description from Rosalie Saunders of what rambling was like at this time.

War!

What must have seemed an idyllic state of affairs for regular ramblers came to an abrupt halt after the excursions that took place on 20 August 1939, on Southern to Bentley, Kingsley Halt and Bordon, and on the LMS to Rickmansworth. As sources of information are contradictory, it is not clear whether the following weekend's trips operated or not due to fears of impending war, but for sure those planned for 3 September, when war was declared, were cancelled. The remaining dates in the published summer programmes, as well as all those that had already been planned for the forthcoming autumn

Two poignant handbills – the final ones to be printed before the outbreak of the Second World War.

and winter, had to be abandoned, and it turned out to be another ten years before the excursions would resume.

Rambling continued around the country, but only on a privately organised and individual basis, and limited to areas that had not been requisitioned or sealed off for military or security purposes (this included most of the coastline). In London, Messrs Page, Grinsell, King and others saw to it that walking boots were kept in action within their respective clubs throughout the war years and beyond. Meanwhile, future organiser George Platt blew up a footbridge near Withyham, East Sussex: this was part of his army duties to make things difficult for an enemy invasion force, and he would joke about it on many post-war occasions when the excursions visited that area.

The re-start

It took several years after the Second World War not only for the railways to recover from the damage they had received but also for the Government of the day to completely reorganise them upon nationalisation in 1948, when the former private companies became regions of what was now British Railways. Meanwhile, J.T. Grinsell and H.E. Page maintained their club programmes, as no doubt did many other rambling clubs around the country.

H.E. Page (now divulging his forename as Hugh but affectionately known to most as 'Pago', as it was written, but pronounced Pargo) was able to re-start ramble excursions on the Southern Region on 3 April 1949 (Easter Sunday) with a special train to Pulborough and Amberley which attracted more than 300 customers – most of them in a motley assortment of whatever gear they could assemble, including hobnail boots, oilskins and enormous war-surplus rucksacks with iron frames. By the early 1950s regular excursions were operating again on both the Southern and Western Regions.

The revival was short-lived though, as the extremely severe winter of 1951-52 led to a grave fuel shortage and cancellation of all but essential traffic of all kinds, including the ramble excursions. However, Prime Minister Winston Churchill issued a directive that railway operators should do all possible to attract maximum traffic, to help revive the economy, and the excursions re-started on the Southern Region in June 1952. But now a certain George Platt was in charge as Pago had taken the opportunity to retire from organising, though he continued as a leader.

The Southern excursions then continued – on a fortnightly basis in summer, monthly in winter – with hardly a break (see 'Disruptions' below) until they were wound up in 2004. Meanwhile, Bob Mulholland was organising the Western Region excursions, though we have little information about dates and destinations at this time.

In October 1954, George Lockie introduced his occasional additional ramblers' excursions by train (sometimes in conjunction with the Railway Enthusiasts Club). Then in October 1955, and more significantly for our story, the ramblers' excursions by coach started.

Soon, as in pre-war days, there were excursions for London ramblers every Sunday and on most public holidays, but the war seemed to have had a dampening effect on both the organisers and the ramblers: there were never again such verve, imagination and stamina in the programmes: no dancing, no night rambles, no Saturday afternoons, no cross-Channel trips.

However, there were some unusual destinations. Some excursions ran far afield to places such as Abergavenny, with buses to take people further into the countryside before they began their rambles back to Abergavenny, or to Chepstow with buses up the Wye valley, the train service having ceased. Buffet cars were provided for some of the longer journeys. An excursion to Shalford on 7 July 1974 included an optional narrow-boat trip on the River Wey.

The large pre-war attendances held up for a while. Sometimes two special trains, each carrying over 500 passengers, were needed for the more popular destinations like Berwick and Polegate: the first went non-stop, the second called at intermediate pick-up points, with leaders travelling on the first train and rearguards on the second train to bring its passengers to the lunch stop. In 1958, the first excursion to the Isle of Wight caught the organisers out when 1,200 people

Coaches ready to take excursionists on from Abergavenny, 5 June 1960.

turned up for the 700 seats available on the special train; those who missed the special train had to travel on the regular service to Portsmouth, where an extra ferry had been organised.

Some excursions caused problems for organisers and railway officials when trains of eight or more carriages ran on lines that were not normally used by such trains, as the locomotives used to pull them were too heavy and the platforms too short; then the locos had to be replaced at some point and the train had to move forward to allow passengers in the back carriages to alight.

A particular bone of contention, though, was the train operators refusal (with some rare exceptions) to reinstate the pre-war concession of travelling out by one line and returning by another, except by buying two expensive single tickets. A more flexible approach would have enabled a much more varied programme.

One of the regular features of train rambles to Wadhurst and Etchingham was a visit to a farm at Earlye run by the Gingell family, who each year welcomed one of the parties to see how their farm was run, followed by afternoon tea in the 15th century farmhouse.

In the summer, an optional evening walk was often offered after tea. Sometimes the return train did not leave the first pick up station until 7 p.m or shortly afterwards, then as pubs did not open until that time on Sundays, a (probably illegal) arrangement was made whereby the landlord had drinks lined up before opening time for the thirsty ramblers to down in the few minutes available before their train departed!

Merry-Makers

In 1971 a programme of rail excursions called Merry-Makers was set up by Percy Danks of British Rail's Midland Region for the general public, and became very popular. Initially they ran mostly on Saturdays – some involved travelling out Friday evening and returning late Saturday evening or early Sunday morning.

Some London ramblers regularly went on Merry-Makers that were not part of the official programme but were sometimes mentioned in the excursion itinerary sheets, with Geoffrey Stevenson being the contact for anyone wishing to join him. (Details of such trips are not included in Appendix A.)

An early one from St Pancras to Manchester (not an 'official' ramblers' excursion) was 'invaded' by ramblers after arrangements had been made for the train to stop at Edale. Over 200 ramblers descended from the train there, leaving very few people on board for Manchester. On the return journey, the driver forgot he was supposed to stop at Edale, screeched to a halt just past the station and reversed back to it. An excursionists' legend has it that Geoffrey Stevenson hooked his walking stick around one of the tail-end buffers and hauled the train back, but this is probably apocryphal!

Once the potential income had been recognised, further Merry-Makers were organised with ramblers in mind, to places like Macclesfield, Prestatyn and even one that went from St Pancras to Weston-super-Mare. Merry-Makers were advertised with either an 'R' or a 'W' against the destinations: R meant there would be led walks from those stations (these trips were sometimes given the soubriquet 'Ramblers' Delight'), whilst if the suffix was W ramblers were expected to make their own arrangements as regards walking in the area. Other regions soon caught on, with Western using the names 'Pied Piper' and 'Suntan Special', but later the Merry-Maker brand was extended to all other regions except Southern, who had coined the term 'Awayday'.

The first Merry-Maker to be used for an 'official' ramblers' excursion went to Matlock on bank holiday Monday 31 May 1971. Initially used for excursion trains only, the name was later applied to special offers on scheduled service trains. Often the number of tickets was limited to one carriage load, when ramblers were strongly advised to buy their tickets well in advance.

Merry-Makers continued to be used for 'official' ramble excursions – the last one mentioned in our records was on 19 September 1982 to Wellington, Shropshire. Gradually the Southern Region's 'Awayday' brand was extended to special offers for leisure journeys throughout the British Rail network, and the Merry-Maker name was dropped. *(As 'Merrymakers', the name was revived in 1996 for several years by the privately-run excursion operator Hertfordshire Railtours.)*

Closures

A sour note amid all this success was the closure of railway lines and stations, including many that had previously been used for the excursions, at an average of about two stations a year since the Second World War. A particularly bad year was 1955, when 11 of those stations shut their gates. Either there were no funds available to reinstate many of the lines that had been destroyed or damaged by enemy action, or they were too uneconomic to maintain, or they fell victim to a policy of closing small stations on some main lines to provide a clearway for express trains.

The closures reached their peak between 1964 and 1968, after the notorious, so-called 'Beeching Axe' fell on most of the country's little branch lines, taking with them at least 57 stations in good rambling country within easy reach of London, which had been regular destinations for these excursions. The choice was substantially reduced, and some regular excursionists became bored with the repetitiveness of the programmes on offer.

Disruptions

Most disruptions were caused by those dreaded **engineering works**! It had to be accepted that they were necessary to keep the network safe, and that they would take place at weekends rather than on busier weekdays – usually on Sundays. During the 1970s there was reasonable notice, which allowed organisers to reschedule destinations, but from the 1980s onwards advance warning was only available a week or so beforehand, by which time it was too late to make alternative arrangements. Works were taking place somewhere nearly every weekend, and they seemed to hit the Sunday ramble excursions far too often. This resulted in revised itineraries and readjustment of planned walks at short notice.

The train excursion that was supposed to go to to Crowborough, Buxted and Uckfield on 24 September 1978 was hit by a double whammy: first, engineering works led to its being replaced by one to Hever, Cowden and Ashurst, then the lack of a guard resulted in the return journey being cancelled. George Platt, with his usual resourcefulness, laid on coaches to carry the 110 ramblers home.

David Horwill was Secretary of the RA Inner London Area Transport Committee (see page 47) during this period and remembers:

"Plod on we did, according to what was there: late starts, rushed morning walks to get to a pub before closing time! And those relying on food at the pub might wonder if they would get any. What seemed quite incredible, though, was the almost total lack of co-ordination between train operators and the bus companies hired to carry passengers between stations. Narrow roads leading to some stations or lack of turning places often meant that the vehicles used could not get close and had to stop some distance away, but passengers were not always informed. Many a time they waited at stations, totally unaware that the bus did not stop there!

"Bus drivers often had no clear directions. If train operators used a bus company that was not local, their drivers were usually ignorant of the area, then ramble party leaders, armed with the appropriate maps, had to direct drivers to the correct destination. Pity the poor passengers who were left to the driver's own devices after the ramblers had alighted!"

Engineering works reached a peak towards the late 1990s, when Network Rail decided that too much maintenance work had been left undone for too long and planned extended periods of disruption (still ongoing some twenty years later). Furthermore, many pubs were turning towards only offering Sunday roasts, with the bar snacks preferred by most ramblers being 'off the menu'. This situation led to a major decision by the Transport Committee for what turned out to be the final season in 2004 – to change to Saturday rambles.

Occasionally the advertised excursions had to be abandoned due to unforeseen circumstances. From time to time there were outbreaks of **foot-and-mouth disease** among livestock in Britain, and despite there being no firm evidence that it can be carried by walkers this resulted in closure of public rights of way in the countryside for extended periods of several months until the outbreak passed. Some local authorities panicked to the extent that they even closed rights of way that had no livestock, and this led to a huge outcry from local businesses that depended on tourism and ramblers for their livelihood. Such outbreaks have occurred in the UK in October 1967, February 2001 and August 2007.

An outbreak obviously severely affects rambling, though it has usually been possible to provide some form of excursion. In 1967 it was possible to use country lanes, but by the later outbreaks they had become too busy and programmes were confined to urban areas or seaside promenades – this provided an opportunity for ramblers to realise that there is in fact some very attractive walking within Greater London.

One well remembered trip to Holmwood and Ockley on 19 November 1967 became notorious for the 'Leith Hill episode'. Tired

A slightly creased photo of a group of ramblers awaiting the homeward train at Chilworth, possibly on 30 July 1967. The central group includes Vanguards Pat Baker, Hazel Cooke, Marie-Hélène Fohr, Jenny Cooke, David Griffin and Howard Johnson.

of walking along country lanes, Bob Goodman led a breakaway party consisting mostly of Vanguards up and down Leith Hill (open to walkers during that foot-and-mouth outbreak) from different directions, and in the misty conditions tried to convince his party that they were climbing different hills!

On 15 September 1968, the planned special train to Gomshall, Chilworth and Shalford was cancelled due to **flooding**, but some ramblers used their initiative to take scheduled trains to Gomshall via Redhill, walked to Shere, then caught a bus to Shalford. They found there were no trains from there so hitched to Guildford for the scheduled train home.

Other disruptions were caused by **rail strikes** in 1965, 1974 and 1982, and a **very heavy snowfall** in 1979. Even then, many ramblers turned up at the departure stations and were led around London's parks and riverside paths. The two trains cancelled due to strikes in 1974 were replaced at short notice by coach excursions.

The so-called 'hurricane' (but more accurately the '**Great Storm**') of the night of 15-16 October 1987 caused considerable damage to trees, resulting in blocked footpaths for several months afterwards, and it was necessary to change planned routes. However, this did result in local authorities making improvements to the footpath network as a result of the substantial funds that were made available by central Government to rectify the damage.

The train excursion to Sevenoaks and Hildenborough scheduled for 19 December 1993 had to be cancelled due to a **suspected bomb on the line**. One of the three leaders, Richard Kendall, travelled down on the replacement bus and led his walk, but most ramblers went either with Geoffrey Stevenson to the Central Royal Parks or with Micky Kohn to Richmond Park and walked there.

3: THE COACH RAMBLES

London Transport had earlier tried an experiment with ramble excursions by coach but they were not well supported and did not continue. But during the early 1950s John Grinsell started some private excursions for his own club, hiring coaches from George Ewer & Co Ltd (then trading as both Grey-Green Coaches and Orange Luxury Coaches) who were later taken over by the Cowie Group of Sunderland, which in turn eventually became part of the nationwide Arriva Group in 1997.

In 1955 John persuaded George Ewer's director Len King (his former collaborator on pre-war train rambles) that it would be a good idea to open up these excursions to the general public. To do this, it was necessary to obtain a bus operator's licence from the Traffic Commissioners for each destination area, specifying the pick-up and set-down points. These were duly granted, and an experimental programme of five trips was organised by the very same Norman Burchill that we encountered previously in this story on an early train excursion back in 1933. Norman organised the programmes until 1966, when Geoffrey Stevenson took over and continued in this role until the last coach excursion in 2000.

The first coach ramble took place on 30 October 1955 to Nettlebed and Henley, with two coaches carrying 57 passengers on parties led by John Grinsell and Hubert Beale. The fare was 7s 6d (37½p) – the equivalent of £6.80 in 2014. By 1957 the programme had increased to 20 and more trips per year. The coaches usually filled the gaps when there was no Southern Region train ramble but they sometimes clashed with excursions on other regions, at least until the programmes were properly co-ordinated by the Transport Committee.

At their peak in the mid 1960s there were well over a hundred ramblers out on the coach excursions, usually requiring at least two and often three or four coaches. The record was 210 on 24 October 1965 to Dover and Deal (always a very popular destination), when five coaches were needed. Yet the coach rambles were never as popular as those by train, for several reasons. As well as the usual stops for a pub lunch and an afternoon tea, it was the practice to include a break on the outward journey, for refreshment and toilets, and as the journey was often slower by coach than train this limited the distance that could be walked; this put off some of the hardier types that frequented the train rambles. Unlike the train rambles, where usually one could just turn up and buy a ticket, you were advised to book ahead for the coaches. It probably didn't help that the destinations were often obscure villages that few had heard of.

However, the coaches offered more flexibility with an infinite variety of destinations not limited to stations, with the added attraction of the coach being available all day to provide transport. In later years, the coach fares were considerably higher than the bargain weekend day returns available on the trains. However, an effort to regain lost passengers was made by reducing the coach fares in 1983.

Originally the coaches departed from Horse Guards Avenue, but heightened security arrangements in the area eventually made this impractical and in1989 they transferred to Victoria Embankment, close to Embankment tube station. According to the direction of travel out of central London, suburban pick-up points were selected from those that were permitted by the local licensing authorities.

Coach excursion organiser Len King (right) with John Jenkins, one of the Commandos organisers (see page 79).

The coach rambles lasted for 45 years without a break, except for the Christmas period. They celebrated their 20th anniversary on 2 November 1975 to Lamberhurst, their 30th on 27 October 1985 to Tenterden, and their 40th on 5 November 1995 to Saffron Walden. Len King organised the coaches (often providing extra ones at very short notice) and looked after the financial side until his death in 1999, after which the coaches were hired from Leaside Travel, another part of the Cowie Group, while Norman Burchill (later Geoffrey Stevenson) organised the destinations, and Harold Lawrence kept the records.

John Grinsell led one of the parties on almost every excursion from the start in 1955 until shortly before his death in 1986, but in later years his walks became more of a 3 or 4 mile stroll, often including a visit to some place of interest such as a stately home in the area, while Geoffrey or another leader from the train rambles (many of them members of the Vanguards Rambling Club) led a longer walk of about 7-8 miles.

Initially, George Ewer operated these excursions as a profit or loss public facility, but when numbers started to drop during the 1970s they insisted that it could only continue on a private hire basis. Len King and Geoffrey Stevenson took this on at their own risk – usually at a small profit (from which they made a donation to the Ramblers' Association) but they had to stand any loss, a situation that became more frequent in later years and eventually led to the demise of the coach excursions. The last one operated on 10 December 2000 to the Whipsnade area.

Other ramblers' excursions by coach

Many other ramblers' excursions by coach were operated from London, but most were privately organised by clubs for members only. However, from 1986 until 1992 the Bucks and West Middlesex Area of the Ramblers' Association ran a monthly trip from spring to autumn that was open to the public. Organised by Diana and Peter Gulland, their main purpose was to draw attention to less well used footpaths in Buckinghamshire beyond the Chilterns. The excursions started at Uxbridge Underground Station, with pick-up points including Amersham, Great Missenden, Wendover, Denham, Chalfont St Peter and Aylesbury.

4: DECLINE AND FALL

In the 1930s, when rambling was at a peak, attendances on the Southern Railway excursions had averaged 600-700, sometimes rising over 1,000, and often with a standby relief train in attendance.

The numbers held up quite well after the war (indeed, on 4 May 1958 an excursion to the Isle of Wight attracted 1,200) but a steady decline soon started. In 1969, in connection with a competition he organised to celebrate his 400th excursion as organiser, George Platt announced that 162,992 people had travelled on them since 1953 – an average of 407 per trip.

When formal recording of attendances by the Transport Committee started in 1975 it was obvious that they were diving into free-fall, as shown by these annual average figures at five-yearly intervals:

Year	Southern	Other regions	Coaches	Overall
1975	143	153	76*	116
1980	132	102	70	102
1985	74	56	47	60
1990	76	57	47	61
1995	35	33	34	34
2000	28	22	24	26
2004	26	23	**	25

* This is the 1976 figure as coach attendances were not reported before that year.
** The coach excursions finished in 2000.

There was a slight halt in the decline during the late 1980s and early 1990s, but Southern Region had pulled the plug in 1975 on special trains for ramblers – unfortunately the finances no longer stacked up. This was despite the goodwill of the railway staff, who had been very sympathetic to the excursions over the decades – indeed, many were ramblers and regular excursionists themselves.

Already by 1973 it had become necessary on some Southern excursions to use scheduled service trains, to which a number of carriages reserved for ramblers had been attached. In 1974 only five of them were special ramblers excursions, and the one to Cooksbridge, Lewes and Glynde on 15 September in that year proved to be the last. A note from George Platt in the itinerary for Hever, Cowden and Ashurst on 15 December 1974, announcing the 1975 programme, stated:

> Due to operational reasons and a declining lack of support, we shall be travelling on ordinary service trains, often slow stopping trains, to serve your favourite stations. In some cases it will be necessary to change trains en route in both directions. Whilst this may not be as convenient as using special trains it is the only alternative to enable the excursions to continue.

Although the 'glory years' were over, the ramble excursions continued to potter along quite nicely for a while, though with much smaller numbers, using scheduled service trains and the special coaches, but something intangible was lost when the special trains ended.

The very low fares that had applied on special trains were no longer available; however, for nearly ten years Southern offered a concession in which the normal day return fare to the nearest station was charged, with onward travel to the further stations in effect being free. But this concession was withdrawn from January 1984, when it became necessary to pay the fare for the furthest station – a situation that penalised those ramblers who would only use the nearer station, but didn't know this until they had studied the day's itineraries. One final concession remained, as Southern agreed to open stations on some dates for the Ramblers' Excursions that were normally closed on Sundays.

It became possible to take advantage of a variety of special fares that were available to the general public, including the Merry-Makers and Awaydays, mentioned earlier. Southern also introduced special low Weekend Awaydays and Seaside Saver Awaydays, which were sometimes used for the ramblers' excursions.

To encourage travellers to travel by train and reduce the impact of the fare increases, British Rail introduced a number of money-saving schemes. Probably the most successful of these was what came to be called 'Persil Vouchers', introduced in the 1980s, with which a free ticket could be purchased for a companion in exchange for tokens from packets of Persil washing powder and other products from the Procter & Gamble stable. Other schemes included the Journey Club Railcard. which enabled passengers to obtain half-price tickets.

For Londoners, a further money-saving arrangement was the Capitalcard, which on payment of the relevant annual fee provided free travel at weekends within Greater London, so that ramble excursionists only had to pay the fare from the outer zone to their destination. From 1986, the over 60s could take advantage of the

Freedom Pass, which allowed them to buy tickets from the Greater London boundary.

Despite these concessions, and a resurgence in rambling as a leisure activity (membership of the Ramblers' Association increased substantially during this period), the excursions were hit by a multitude of whammies:

- The increasing success of the RA's local groups in offering led walks for members. Many of these groups were based in London's suburbs, with the result that potential excursionists living in those areas preferred to walk with their local group.
- The rising cost of public transport: people who could well remember paying less than £1 for the return fare back in the 1960s were now being asked to pay up to £20, and sometimes more.
- The depressed state of public transport, with little being spent due to the uncertainties of privatisation.
- The increasing use of cars to reach walk destinations.
- Closure of lines and stations resulting in a more limited choice of destinations, so that many excursionists became bored with the restricted options available.
- Better guidebooks and maps for walkers were being published, and many people who wanted to walk in the countryside were becoming more confident about finding the way and making their own arrangements, whether as individuals, families or informal groups of friends.
- The increasing number of ways in which ramblers were encouraged to walk independently, including named trails and routes published in books and outdoor magazines.
- Withdrawal in 1983 of publicity paid for by the British Railways Board.
- Increase in railway engineering works leading to frequent disruptions to schedules.
- Inappropriate or limited food choice at lunch pubs, and more restrictions on eating one's own food.
- Restricted availability of afternoon tea stops.

- A poor image of ramblers and rambling among the general public, not helped by the increasing average age and old-fashioned attire of many regular excursionists.
- An ageing clientèle dropping out and not being replaced.
- Plummeting attendances often meant that only one party could be offered, with the result that many excursionists became frustrated at the lack of choice.

In the light of all this, it is hardly surprising that by 1977 the average attendance had dropped from the upper hundreds at their peak to 138 on Southern and 94 on other regions. So in 1978 a working party was set up by the Transport & Publicity Sub-committee of the Ramblers' Association's Southern Area (later becoming the Transport Committee of the Inner London Area) to consider ways of improving attendances. Its members were David Sharp, Edwin Lambert, Bill Craies and Graham Collett.

But despite several measures and experiments tried by the sub-committee, including special rambles for families, and a slight improvement in 1989-1990, the long-term decline could not be halted and the downward spiral continued.

Occasionally the figure topped 100, but the last time this occurred was 29 April 1990 by train to Hollingbourne and Harrietsham. The last excursion to reach 50 went on 15 September 1996 to Eynsford, Shoreham and Otford (though a later one in May 2003 reached 55 with the help of members of a local RA group).

After privatisation in 1996, the new train operators refused to provide free survey tickets, or even to pay for any publicity. Most leaders and rearguards offered to pay their own survey expenses, but the only way people could find details of the excursions was by reading *Sunday Rambler* (later retitled *London Rambler*, and provided free or on subscription to anyone interested) and *South Eastern Rambler* (now *South East Walker*, the regional journal sent to most RA members in south-east England).

With little publicity, and despite herculean efforts by the Transport Committee, in effect the train rambles became a closed shop, known only to the faithful core. The official train rambles struggled on with a couple of dozen regulars, but the writing was on the wall. The lowest ever attendance of eight was recorded on 25 February 2001 to Hastings, though this was during an outbreak of foot-and-mouth disease when rambling in the countryside was severely restricted.

All this at a time when public rambles known as Saturday Strolls and Waterside Walks within Greater London, organised by the RA's Inner London Area, were proving highly successful.

The coach rambles had a brief resurgence in 1982 when the number of passengers carried rose slightly to an average of nearly 70 per trip. But they gradually dwindled and it then became a struggle to fill just one coach. An appeal for more support in the January 1998 issue of *London Rambler* had little effect. Then in May 1999, after 44 years of organising coach excursions, Len King died and Geoffrey Stevenson carried the flag alone for another 18 months. The final ramblers' excursion by coach ran on 10 December 2000 to Whipsnade, Kensworth, Caddington and Stockwood Park in Bedfordshire, when a short speech was made to 34 ramblers by John Grinsell's daughter, Celia.

To fill the gaps left by the demise of the coach excursions, additional ones by train were inserted on some dates. Also for a while Geoffrey Stevenson organised day trips by train on the other gap dates to regular rambling haunts in the countryside, or sometimes within Greater London. Described as 'Geoffrey Stevenson Sunday Specials' and patronised by many of the regular excursionists, they were not regarded as official excursions and their attendances were not recorded by the Transport Committee. They ceased in September 2002 as Geoffrey was unable to continue organising them.

By now, due to a lack of leaders, often only one party could be organised, and in many cases that had to be led by the organiser. But as so few people were travelling it was hardly worth offering more.

In their final year, 2004, the decision was taken to switch the train rambles to Saturdays, mainly to minimise disruption by engineering works, but also to provide a better menu choice at pubs, which were increasingly offering little more than traditional roast dinners on Sundays. To avoid clashing with the Saturday Strolls they would take place on alternate weeks. Whilst this led to fewer engineering disruptions and better menu choice, the writing was already on the wall for the future of the train excursions.

Transport Committee Secretary David Horwill had decided not to continue as overall organiser beyond the end of 2004, and as nobody came forward to take charge of a programme for 2005, the public excursions came to a complete halt on 18 December 2004 with a trip to Chelsfield.

Yet the indefatigable Geoffrey Stevenson refused to be beaten: he said he would lead six walks and see how they went. The faithful core (two or three dozen) were determined to continue, and although he is no longer with us the walks that Geoffrey started were still running at the time of writing, now known as 'Geoff's Jaunts' in his memory – see page 84.

It seems that the social phenomenon of the ramblers' excursions from London, which lasted 72 years from 1932 to 2004, was closely linked to the lifespans of their most illustrious organisers. Although Hugh E. Page's life was ended prematurely by a road accident in 1958, the others died of natural causes: John Grinsell in 1986, George Platt in 1998 and Len King in 1999. Geoffrey Stevenson soldiered on for a few years after the demise, until he too was taken from us in 2010.

Many others made substantial contributions, but this book should be considered as a lasting tribute to those five great men of the London rambling scene.

5: ORGANISATION

The Transport Committee
The ramblers' excursions by train originally had no official standing within the Ramblers' Association. Indeed, the RA had barely been established (as the National Council of Ramblers' Federations) when the excursions started – they were originally a collaboration between competing railway companies and individual organisers. As a result,

there was no attempt to co-ordinate dates at first and there were often two or more excursions on the same day during the 1930s.

After the war, by the time the excursions had properly re-established themselves in the 1950s it had become apparent that the number of potential excursionists had fallen, and that it was now necessary for a degree of co-ordination between what were now regions of British Railways. It seems likely that the organisers of the train and coach excursions achieved this on an informal basis at first, but in June 1974 a formal co-ordinating committee was formed, overseen by the Southern Area of the Ramblers' Association.

Initially known as the Transport & Publicity Sub-Committee, and meeting six times a year, its first members were Ted Cutter (chairman), Michael Kohn (secretary), Graham Collett, Howard Gutteridge, George Platt, Bill Ramsey, Brian Reader, Geoffrey Stevenson, Ken Thornton and Andrew Ward.

Certain committee members were tasked with organising the excursions: initially they were George Platt for the Southern Region trains, Graham Collett jointly with Andrew Ward for 'Other Regions' trains, and Geoffrey Stevenson for the coaches.

The Committee systematically minuted attendances on each excursion, which had previously only been mentioned sporadically. Though it seems they were often 'guestimates' as so many were round figures! Eventually Geoffrey Stevenson produced a tally counter (always referred to as his 'clicker'), which enabled more accurate figures to be provided.

In 1984 the vast Southern Area was split into smaller ones based largely on counties, including one for London, later becoming Inner London, for which the functions of transport and publicity were given to separate sub-committees. Organisation of the excursions then became the responsibility of what was always referred to as the Transport Committee. The meetings were held at the RA's offices in Vauxhall, London, until 1997, then at Bridget Harper's home near Earls Court. It continued to meet regularly until December 2004, when the organised excursions were wound up. Michael Kohn and

Geoffrey Stevenson were still members so had each given well over 30 years' service. Others at that final meeting were David Horwill (chairman and secretary), Brenda Horwill, Bridget Harper, Eliana and Terry Davidson and Arthur Reed. After the final meeting, Bridget very kindly treated them all to a meal at a local restaurant.

Allocation of dates

By the 1960s a pattern had developed in which train rambles would use special trains on the Southern Region on alternate Sundays, since most of the good walking country accessible by train from London lies in that direction. The intervening Sundays were taken up by either a train ramble on one of the other regions, using scheduled service trains, or a coach ramble. Occasionally an excursion would use the London Underground. Additional excursions were arranged on most public holidays.

The trains would usually depart from the London terminus around 10 to 10.30 a.m. An earlier time was sometimes necessary for longer journeys, but was not normally practical due to the late Sunday starts of the Underground and suburban train services, and those living in the suburbs needed time to come up. The Southern excursions usually called at places like Clapham Junction, East Croydon, Bromley South or Surbiton. The coaches usually departed from Horseguards Avenue (later Embankment) at 9.30, with two or three suburban pick-up points.

Despite their best efforts to co-ordinate, there seems to have been some dissension amongst Transport Committee members at times. George Platt got very worked up about an excursion planned to Edale in the Peak District for November 1973, which he thought too late for a high moorland area, and tried very hard to dissuade people from going on it. Competing official excursions were organised on at least two occasions, though this did not seem to affect the attendances: on 12 May 1974, Southern's to Canterbury East attracted 179 while the Merry-Maker to Hope and Edale got 185; and on 1 June 1975 a coach trip to New Romney ran in opposition to Southern's excursion to Holmwood.

During the 1970s there was criticism from certain quarters about the repetitive nature of the Southern destinations. Some leaders became bored with being asked to repeat previous walks on Southern and deserted them for the coaches and Other Regions. When the Merry-Maker excursions were in their prime in the late 1970s, many regular ramblers took advantage of the more interesting destinations they offered on Saturdays rather than travel on Southern's Sunday ones.

Preparation

It was the organiser's responsibility to find a number of leaders for each excursion, then the leaders had to find what was always called on these excursions a 'rearguard' (more commonly known elsewhere as a 'backmarker'). On the day, the rearguard would have to close gates, ensure that all the ramblers were accounted for and let the leader know if any were having trouble keeping up, or even take over if the leader was ill or incapacitated, or failed to turn up, or simply needed a break. Most leaders worked with a regular and trusted rearguard.

A month or two before each excursion, the organiser would suggest to leaders at which stations to start and end their ramble, and possibly which pub to stop at for lunch, and in summer where to stop for afternoon tea – this was to ensure that everyone did not follow the same or similar routes. The distance was up to the leaders, but generally between 8 and 15 miles, depending on the time of year and train times, and it was the aim to offer a variety of distances.

The leaders and rearguards would then carry out what was always referred to on these excursions as a 'survey' of their planned route (though the term 'reconnaissance' or 'recce' is more commonly used elsewhere) to check that the paths to be followed were free of impediment and establish whether the pub and tea stop were suitable and willing to accept the party. On completion of the survey, leaders were required to provide route details to the organiser for inclusion in the 'itinerary sheets' that were handed out on the day. If there were problems with the route, the organiser or leader would try to sort them out before the day of the excursion.

For the train rambles, until 1993 the operating company provided leaders and rearguards with a free ticket, which they could use on both the survey and the excursion itself. After that, expenses were not covered, either for the survey or on the day. For the coaches, leaders and rearguards got a free seat on the excursion and their travel expenses for the survey were reimbursed.

In later years it became increasingly difficult to get enough leaders and rearguards to offer a good choice of walks. The lack of leaders from among the excursionists' ranks was eased to some extent by offers from RA local groups to lead walks when excursions visited their neck of the woods.

Following a dreadful accident in 1976, in which five members of Kettering & District Rambling Club were killed while walking along a country lane with no pavement, the fear of litigation grew and it became necessary for all leaders and rearguards to be RA members so that they were covered by its insurance.

On the day
It was not normally necessary to book in advance for the trains (though there were some exceptions including some of the Merry-Makers) but it was advisable to reserve a seat for the coaches. On boarding the train or coach, ramblers were handed an itinerary sheet with details of each of the walks on offer: route, distance, pub and afternoon tea stops and names of leader and rearguard.

At their peak, a choice of up to nine itineraries was offered on the trains, and those that joined them were always known as 'parties'. The coaches usually had just two but occasionally three parties. During the journey, the organiser or assistants would ask each rambler which party they intended to join. If it seemed that too many people wanted to join a particular party, some would then be asked to switch to another one. Some (especially clubs travelling on the train) might say they would do their own walk.

On special trains, the organiser and assistants had a compartment to themselves for use as an 'office'. The leaders and rearguards were also allocated their own space, though many preferred to sit with their party members.

Each leader was provided with a wooden bat, on which the party number was written. On arrival at the starting station, leaders or rearguards would hold up their bat, and call out 'Party number one' etc, then the ramblers would gravitate towards their chosen party.

Although many ramblers prefer to picnic, a lunchtime pub stop was traditional on these excursions – this helped to improve the image of ramblers by contributing to the local economy. However, there were times when few pubs provided more than the bare minimum of food – nuts, crisps and maybe sandwiches if you were lucky. So many ramblers took their own food, which they were asked to consume outside the pub. It is ironic that pubs vastly improved their catering towards the end of these excursions!

Leaders were encouraged to foster good relationships with pub landlords by asking ramblers to remove or cover muddy boots before entering, not to eat their own food inside, return empty glasses to the counter and replace tables and chairs in their original position.

An afternoon tea stop was an important feature of summer excursions, and in their early days there were plenty of facilities, not only at dedicated tea-rooms and tea-gardens. Some pubs would do it, and often the local women's institute would be very willing to provide it in the village hall. The number that the tea stop could cater for was indicated in the day's itinerary sheet and there were times when some ramblers had to switch to another party or go without.

The organisers

Of course, the excursions would not have taken place without the hard work and dedication of many voluntary organisers over the years, but among them strode five giants: Messrs H.E. Page, J.T.

Grinsell, L.R. King, G. Platt and A.G. Stevenson. The contributions made by these men cannot be overestimated. Some idea can be inferred from the number of times their names appear in Appendix A (see page 2) as organisers and leaders: Stevenson 1,133, King 726 and Platt 708, while Grinsell (727) and Page (352) are grossly under-represented as so many of their dates have been lost. It is worth noting here too that Michael Kohn made a significant contribution – he is mentioned 525 times.

The Magnificent Five

<u>Hugh E. Page</u> (1879-1959)
Hugh Edward Page was born in Amersham, Bucks, in 1879. Affectionately known as 'Pago' (pronounced 'Pargo'), he was the first organiser of these excursions, from 1932 to 1952, and often led one of the parties.

He was Honorary Transport Secretary of the National Federation of Rambling Clubs (as it was then known), secretary of the North Finchley Rambling Club and founder in 1926 of the Connoisseur Rambling Club. He also wrote a series of books of suggested rambles for the Great Western Railway which remained in print long after the railways were nationalised in 1948 – second-hand copies can still be widely found on the internet, including Amazon and eBay. They covered South Devon, Cornwall, the Cotswolds, the Chilterns, Somerset, the Cambrian Coast and the Wye Valley.

During the Second World War, Pago managed to maintain weekly rambles for the Connoisseurs. In 1952, at the age of 73, he took advantage of an enforced eight-month halt to the excursions, brought about by a fuel crisis, to hand over the reins to George Platt.

Tragically, Pago died after a road accident in August 1959 while surveying for a ramble in the Chilterns that would have celebrated his 80th birthday. A fund was started for a tribute to him and a memorial seat was installed at Toy's Hill in Kent and handed over to the National Trust at a ceremony on 23 October 1960; a special extra excursion was organised for this event with three parties approaching the seat from different directions.

John T. Grinsell (1905-1986)

Born on 9 February 1905, the son of a silversmith, John Tabor Grinsell was educated at Hurstpierpoint public school. With the South Downs close at hand, this was where he discovered his love of walking, though until his early 20s he was also a keen cyclist. He founded the Sussex Pathfinders Rambling Club and by the early 1930s was organising Wednesday afternoon rambles for the Southern Railway into the South Downs from Brighton and other south coast towns. He is thought to have been the first person to have organised conducted rambles for the general public – before this they had been organised by clubs for members only.

Walking became John's *raison d'être*, though he earned a living as a fish salesman, and later as a factory hand. After attending that first 'mystery excursion' from Paddington in 1932, he was a leader on the second ever Southern Railways excursion in May 1932 and led on nearly every weekend thereafter almost until he died.

John persuaded the LMS and LNER to run excursions north of the Thames, which were nominally organised by Pago at first, but John led on them and in 1933 took over as official organiser on the LMS, with Len King as his assistant, and in 1934 likewise on the LNER. He also put on rambling breaks and holidays for the LMS in the Lake District and Rutland.

During the war he formed Grinsell's Rambling Club, and every Sunday except one, together with Len King, kept its members' boots pounding away wherever they could get to. Soon afterwards he organised various train rambles on British Rail's Eastern and Midland Regions before moving on to become very much involved with the coach excursions.

There was friendly rivalry between Messrs Page and Grinsell in the pre-war years, when they were both organising excursions on the same dates: Page to the south and Grinsell to the north. At this time there was enough interest to justify such profusion, but this happy state of affairs was brought to an end by the war, and afterwards the dates for the 'official' ramblers excursions were co-ordinated.

In 1955 John was instrumental in establishing the coach rambles. Having successfully organised some for his own club earlier, he persuaded his great friend and fellow club member, Len King, who happened to be a director of George Ewer coaches, to start a programme of excursions for the general public.

On almost every weekend, John was to be found leading one of the parties on a ramble excursion by train or coach. He must have led on something like 500 coaches, and on the excursion to Swanage on 24 May 1970 it was announced on the itinerary sheets that this would be his 300th as a leader on the trains. So by the time he retired from leading in 1981 it seems likely that he had led well over a thousand times on both trains and coaches – and that excludes those he led for Grinsell's Rambling Club during the war and at other times.

John is fondly remembered by excursionists as an avuncular, genial and quietly-spoken man with a ready smile. On the coaches he would be sitting by the door, accompanied by his wife, Winifred (but known to all as 'Winsome'), whom he met through rambling – they

Photos of John Grinsell are hard to come by. This one was taken on a coach ramble to Maldon, Essex.

married in 1941. His memory failed in later years – he would usually recognise a face but could never remember the name! As passengers boarded the coach he would warmly greet them and say, 'Hello, er, no don't tell me, I know your name, wait a minute....' but he usually failed to place it.

John was made a Vice President of the Southern Area of the Ramblers' Association, and when he could no longer take part in the excursions he followed intently their activities right up to the day of his death. No one could have given more time and effort than John to making available to everyone the pleasures of walking in the countryside. He died after a stroke on 3 May 1986, aged 81. A memorial seat and fountain were installed in his memory at the National Trust's Wakehurst Place (near Ardingly in Sussex), of which he was particularly fond, and the coach ramble on 13 June 1987 took place in John's memory to include a visit there. It seems that the fountain has since been removed for health and safety reasons, but the NT have said they hope to restore it.

John's daughter Celia was an occasional excursionist and travelled on the Christmas vacations that he organised for Grinsell's Rambling Club. On one of these, to Gloucester in 1962, she met David Short; they married in 1966 and have three sons.

Len King (1911-1999)
Born in east London on 8 May 1911, Leonard Robert King was an accountant and auditor by profession, but his warm-heartedness and helpfulness resulted in offers to become a director of two of his client companies: the George Doland chain of clothing shops and, most appropriately for our story, the George Ewer Group of coach operators, trading principally as Grey-Green and Orange Luxury Coaches.

Len was a keen walker and a fellow-member of the Sussex Pathfinders with his great friend, John Grinsell. Together with John, he took part in the early ramblers' excursions by train and became a regular leader – one of the youngest, in his early 20s. After the success of the Southern Railway's ramblers' excursions, he was invited by John Grinsell to assist him in organising excursions for the LNER and LMS, which they did together until the outbreak of the Second World War.

During the war, Len was in a reserved occupation as a transport organiser, but he continued to help with organising and leading weekly rambles and occasional holidays for Grinsell's Rambling Club. Afterwards, it took some time for the 'official' ramblers' excursions to get going again, especially on what were now the Eastern and London Midland Regions of British Railways. So John and Len continued running private excursions by coach for the club until, in 1955, John suggested that they should be made available to the public and Len persuaded the George Ewer Group to co-operate.

Len was the treasurer of Grinsell's Rambling Club, also for some years the auditor for the Ramblers' Association's Southern Area. He handled the financial side of the coach excursions and travelled on nearly all of them, usually accompanied by his wife, Annette. They met in 1954 when Annette, having just bought a car, was trying it out around the estate where she lived in Woodcote, Epsom. The car ran out of fuel and happened to come to a halt outside Len's house. He ran out to help....and four years later as man and wife they moved into the bungalow that was to become a well known address on the coach handbills, Robin Hill in Riverside Drive, Esher, which they shared until Len died of pneumonia on 29 May 1999, aged 88. In one capacity or another he had worked on behalf of his fellow ramblers for almost 65 years.

Annette arranged for an additional plaque commemorating Len to be added to John Grinsell's seat at Wakehurst Place, so that they can be remembered together.

George Platt (1912-1998)

An almost exact contemporary of Len King, George Platt was a mercurial character who (for the majority of surviving excursionists) was the embodiment of the train rambles. He courted controversy and regular excursionists either loved him or loathed him.

Born in Cheshire in 1912, George served for a while in the Scots Guards then came to work in London in 1937. He started going on the train excursions in 1938 but when war broke out was recalled to the Scots Guards. One of his duties was to make things difficult for an enemy invasion force, and he had to blow up a particular footbridge near Withyham, East Sussex. For years afterwards it was impossible to cross there, and this became a standing joke to which George referred in the excursion itineraries.

Returning to the ramble excursions as a leader when they restarted in 1949, George clearly made an impression because in 1952 Pago handed him the Southern Region reins. During the 30 years from 1952 to 1982 he organised some 700 Southern train excursions, travelling on all of them except two: one in 1953 due to illness and one in 1968 when he accepted an opportunity to sail to Ireland on the liner Queen Elizabeth.

George was aided and abetted by a handful of stewards who obeyed his every command, including Bob Mulholland (who had himself organised excursions earlier) and the rather abruptly-spoken Bill Standing. Their tasks included distributing the ramble itineraries on the train, then finding out which parties they wanted to join, if necessary asking people to choose another if their first choice was oversubscribed. Another of George's henchmen was a gentleman commonly known as 'Jaws' whose only function seemed to be to reinforce George's commands. Even when wrong, George found a way of making out that he was right, but though his overbearing nature and bluster led to some hilarity among the ramblers, it has to be said that he organised the excursions with military efficiency. For example, some destinations had platforms that were shorter than the trains, and George organised the parties so that they were in the right carriages to alight at their station.

Perhaps George's supreme moment of glory came on 4 May 1958, an excursion to the Isle of Wight, when 1,200 ramblers turned up for a train with just 700 seats. He calmly arranged for the overflow to travel down on a service train, and on the way down to Portsmouth

George and Bridie Platt on their wedding day in 1951.

(with the help of the conductor and Southern's communication system) arranged an extra ferry to Ryde and two extra trains from there to Ventnor, plus a relief special train for the return journey to London.

George was fond of celebrations. Soon after taking over from Pago, he organised a special Coronation Day excursion on 2 June 1953 (a Tuesday) to Berwick and Polegate. On 28 May 1972 (Berwick and Polegate again) he celebrated his 20th year of organising. He got very excited about unusual destinations, always saying in advance notices "This is one excursion you must not miss!"

George's often abrasive manner could upset people. In 1969 he was brought up before the RA Southern Area Executive Committee to answer what seems to have been an over-the-top three-page complaint from a Mr P. Clarke, who was dissatisfied about a short delay on the return journey from Swanage and Corfe Castle on 6 April and seems to have received short shrift from George. This was blown up out of all proportion, with insults and accusations flying in all directions, and some members of the committee (whom George had already upset) seeing this as an opportunity to depose him. But somehow George survived and continued organising for another 13 years.

It seems that one bone of contention was to describe himself as Honorary Transport Secretary of the RA Southern Area (a title that Pago had used), which was never authorised by the area's committee. Indeed, Norman Burchill (see below) also had this title, so it is not surprising that there was ill-feeling.

He was not amused on the excursion to Wadhurst and Etchingham on 15 June 1969, when he was misinformed, as a joke apparently, that one of the rearguards had failed to turn up, and he wasted much time trying to organise a replacement, with three leaders vying for the services of two rearguards.

George was rarely known to actually join the walkers, but continued on the train, which he claimed was to 'ensure the return reservations' (though it was alleged that this involved rather lengthy pub visits) until it was time for the return journey. His wife, Bridget (known as Bridie, née Melican), whom he had married in 1951, often accompanied him and seemed to exercise a restraining influence. However, on the excursion to Rye and Winchelsea on 29 March 1970, George and Bridie took over party number one from the hospitalised Ron Harmer, and on 26 October 1975 to Burgess Hill and Hassocks Bridie acted as rearguard for Bridget Harper.

George got very worked up over the Merry-Maker excursion to Edale on 4 November 1973, which had been organised by Arthur Hack and was therefore not his responsibility. Nevertheless, he distributed a note on his excursion to Crowborough and Buxted on 7 October strongly advising people 'not to take part in this most ill advised excursion' due to the short daylight hours and difficult terrain. It may have been sensible advice, but around 160 people ignored it and joined the excursion. As far as is known, no ramblers came to any harm, but it caused much bad feeling among the Transport Committee and especially to Arthur, who was very ill at the time.

George became more cantankerous as he grew older – maybe the strain of organising was taking its toll. He found it difficult to retain existing leaders and recruit new ones, despite increasingly desperate appeals in the ramble itinerary sheets. The author remembers attending a meeting organised by George at the Albert pub in Victoria Street on 13 January 1975, to which potential leaders had been invited to find out what was involved. He emphasised that, if leaders couldn't sort out the walk on their first survey, they would be expected to go a second time, and a third time if necessary.... The meeting was not a great success!

In 1980 George became much involved with the campaign against the construction of the Brighton Bypass, especially how it would affect the South Downs at Patcham, and he urged excursionists to make their own personal protest. George had a way of saying 'Patcham' in his strong Cheshire accent that succinctly described his strong feelings about the scheme.

George could be very difficult to work with and made the Transport Committee meetings a nightmare for a while, but by 1982 he had effectively been ousted as the Southern Region organiser. Making the best of it, in the itinerary for the excursion to Sevenoaks on 8 November 1981, he announced that, approaching his 70th birthday, he felt the time was right to hand over the reins to a younger person, but that he was willing to carry on through 1982 if necessary to give his successor time to acclimatise. Yet even this apparently straightforward action led to acrimony: George wanted to choose his successor but the Committee insisted that they should do this; then George refused to hand over his paperwork on how to organise the excursions, but the Committee managed without.

Before retiring, George produced a celebratory document about the excursions entitled 'Fifty Glorious Rambling Years from 1932 to

61

1982', including a reminder that, during his 30-year watch he had organised over 700 excursions.

Despite his foibles, George was highly regarded and held in great affection by most ramblers. He was invited to become the first chairman of the newly formed Kingston & District Group of the Ramblers' Association in 1964, and on the excursion to Yarmouth and Freshwater on 7 June 1977 he and Bridie were presented with a tankard and pendant to mark the 25th anniversary of his organising career. After stepping down as organiser, George became active in the Chums Rambling Club and served as their chairman, and in early 1983 a collection was taken for him on excursions and this resulted in him being presented with an electronic chess set.

George died aged 85 in 1998. He survived Bridie by just a few weeks; indeed, he attended her funeral in a wheelchair, accompanied by a nurse. Afterwards, at a pub, he had to be fed through a tube, but the nurse poured a glass of whisky through it, then wiped the glass with a napkin, which she then touched to his lips.

Geoffrey Stevenson (1933-2010)
Though coming onto the scene much later than those mentioned above, of all the organisers Geoffrey arguably contributed most to the cause of rambling in southern England. He was passionate about walking, kind and caring, small of stature and timid of bearing, but could pack a verbal punch when his dander was up!

Arthur Geoffrey Stevenson was born in North Middlesex Hospital at Edmonton, London N18, on 26 September 1933, just over a year after our excursions started. He did not care for 'Arthur', preferring 'Geoffrey' but always 'Geoff' to his friends. He lived almost all his life in Palmers Green, but for three years during the Second World War was evacuated to live with his aunt and uncle in Gloucestershire, where he first encountered field paths and his 'love affair' with maps started.

When sister Kathleen was born, though just 11 years old he loved to take her out in a pram around Palmers Green and Edmonton, and would often get completely separated from their mother. He spent all his working life in the publishing business, at first with Iliffe & Sons until they were taken over by the International Publishing Corporation. They allocated him to magazines that were totally inappropriate – *Nursing Mirror* then *Yachting World* – where he handled classified advertising.

In the early 1950s he did two years' National Service in the Royal Army Pay Corps at Wootton in Northamptonshire. Much to everyone's surprise, while there he got into a fight, received a black eye and missed his passing out parade!

Geoffrey's main interest was the countryside and it was not long before he discovered the ramblers' excursions. There seems to be some confusion about which was actually his first excursion but it seems likely to have been on Easter Sunday 9 April 1955 to Billingshurst, Pulborough and Amberley. It was not long before he started to lead – the first record we have being on 3 August 1959 on a Western Region excursion to Wantage.

Geoffrey always particularly enjoyed the coach excursions and when Norman Burchill died in 1965 he took over their organisation, jointly with Len King, continuing in this role until they finished in 2000. He did not get on with George Platt, however, and athough he travelled on the Southern excursions, as far as we know never led on them until after George had retired.

For many years Geoffrey organised (and mostly led) a series of half a dozen short rambles over the Christmas and New Year period within Greater London, which became known as the Yuletide Rambles (see page 83).

From 1993 onwards, in the absence of any other offers, the indefatigable Geoffrey also took over the 'Other Regions' (north of the Thames) train excursions, and often found himself organising three or even four consecutive excursions. When the coaches finished at the end of 2000, some of their dates were replaced by official 'Other Regions' excursions – organised by Geoffrey – and where gaps still remained, determined that the faithful regulars should not be deprived of their Sunday ramble, he put on his own Sunday Specials.

With his stalker's hat and trademark walking stick, Geoffrey endeared himself to regular excursionists, earning himself the nickname 'Geoff o'Stick'. Whenever anything blocked a right of way,

Geoff o'Stile!

Geoffrey Stevenson demonstrates his remarkable technique for dealing with stiles, on a coach excursion to New Alresford and Cheriton (9 March 1975).

he would scream and use his stick in the manner of the bayonet charge he had learned in the army, before enthusiastically slashing at the offending nettles or brambles – ramblers in his way would quickly disperse!

He was notorious for finding the muddiest walks in Essex and often wore wellingtons. In due course, he became a member of (or rather was absorbed into) the Vanguards (see page 78), and was a regular on the Commando Footpath Clearances (see page 80). And as if all this was not enough, he co-ordinated many visits by excursionists to concerts, theatre, opera, old silent movies and evenings of transport films.

Geoffrey was also an enthusiastic activist on behalf of the Ramblers' Association. His involvement goes back to at least 1958 when he was writing in the RA national magazine as 'District Correspondence Secretary' of what was then known as the Southern Area, coordinating the efforts of local footpath secretaries and encouraging members to send in reports of path problems. He joined the Southern (later Inner London) Area Transport Committee at its inception in 1974 and remained until it was wound up in 2004.

He always pressed the case for good rail access to country stations – especially at weekends and off-peak times – and was a key player in the battle to prevent the withdrawal of Sunday train services from a large number of stations in the south-east at a time of government cutbacks, coming up with some useful suggestions to keep as many stations open as possible.

Geoffrey's love of maps resulted in spending much of his spare time and even holidays in libraries that had original copies of the local 'definitive map', which showed all identified public rights of way. Together with David Rogerson of the Vanguards, and using coloured pencils (green for footpaths, purple for bridleways, red for byways), and writing the parish reference number alongside, they laboriously marked up Geoff's copies of the 1:25,000 'Pathfinder' maps so that eventually he built up a complete record of the rights of way network for many counties in southern England, from Devon to Norfolk. This became a valuable resource for RA activists objecting to closures and diversions, and woe betide any farmer who tried to prevent Geoffrey from following any route that he knew was a right of way!

Less well known, but no less importantly, Geoffrey carried out research work for various RA Areas. Ian Mitchell of Norfolk Area recalls that he became interested in assisting with claims for rights of way by looking up particular documents that were only available in the National Archives at Kew. This was particularly useful for RA activists based some distance from London, saving time and expense.

One way in which Geoffrey ingeniously proved a right of way was through the Ordnance Survey namebooks, in which the OS had justified a particular spelling on its six inch to one mile maps of 1900. He combed the 1:25,000 maps for named 'white roads' and tracks, then at Kew looked at the OS namebook for each area and took a copy of pages in which the description said that the roads or tracks were public. He discovered another cunning ruse when he learned that the 1910 Finance Act detailed how public rights of way affected the value of specified parcels of land, and was able to identify many 'lost' footpaths and bridleways by this means.

Geoffrey's work on behalf of the RA was recognised with the presentation of a certificate of achievement by Chief Executive Officer Tom Franklin at the Inner London Area AGM in 2009. This was timely, as Geoffrey had not much longer to live, having developed cancer of the throat, and spent his last days back in North Middlesex Hospital, where he was was born.

Geoffrey loved organ music, and regularly attended concerts all over London but especially those at his local venue, Alexandra Palace. He had hoped to attend a recital there by his great friend and professional organist, Colin Walsh, but was too ill to go – it was the day before he died. So another organist friend, David Liddle, who was there, got special permission to record the recital and, together with Roger Kemp, took the CD for Geoffrey to hear. David asked if he had enjoyed the recording but he was heavily drugged and too ill to speak. He just took David's hand, and David told Roger afterwards that he was amazed at the strength of his grip. Later that day, one of his regular rearguards, Andrew Ward, and another friend, Barbara Marsh, took a CD of classical music, which Geoffrey happily listened to, then quietly slipped away, on 16 July 2010, aged 76.

The funeral at Islington Crematorium was attended by over a hundred relatives and friends, who dispersed afterwards to the sound of 'The Happy Wanderer'. As Geoffrey had said himself not long before, he was going to 'that great ramble in the sky'. Despite (or maybe because of) its reputation for muddy fields, it was always believed that Essex was Geoffrey's favourite walking area, and after his death friends paid to have part of a new Woodland Trust property near Hainault Forest in that county dedicated to his memory.

Geoffrey must have organised and led over a thousand walks for the ramblers' excursions over the years, but in his modest way made less of it than the rumbustious George Platt. When the coach rambles ceased he continued more informally with his Saturday country walks known to many as Geoff's Jaunts (see page 84).

See also the many memories of Geoffrey in Part 2: Reminiscing.

Other organisers

The ramble excursions owe so much to those five men, but many others played a significant role.

Whilst not actually an organiser, as he was instrumental in setting up the excursions something should be said here about **Petre Mais** (1885-1975), as he preferred to be called (Petre being the Romanian equivalent of Peter), though usually formally referred to as S.P.B. Mais. At first a teacher, then a journalist and broadcaster, he took up writing books and is thought to have written over 200, mostly about travel and walking. During the winter of 1933-1934 he broadcast a series from the United States entitled *A Modern Columbus*, an idea that was taken up after the the Second World War by Alistair Cooke, as *Letter from America*. Mais was already well known before the war but became a household name through wartime broadcasts on his popular *On the Kitchen Front* radio programme. On 4 January 1960 he was Roy Plomley's castaway on the BBC radio programme, *Desert Island Discs* – possibly the only ramblers' excursionist to achieve this distinction – so far!

After helping Hugh Page to set up the Southern excursions in 1932, Mais accompanied some of them until at least 1934, and no doubt the inclusion of a celebrity name in the programmes helped get them off the ground. Despite his fame and prolific output, he died relatively poor.

Norman Burchill (1896-1965) was a leader on the early excursions (his name appears as 'Mr N.A. Burchill' on a handbill for an excursion to Ongar on 27 August 1933). Some time after the war he became Transport Secretary of the RA's Southern Area, and organised the coach excursions, jointly with Len King, from their inception in 1955 until his death aged 69 in 1965.

George Lockie (1908-1988) organised occasional ramblers' excursions between 1954 and 1960, which were additional to those promoted by the Southern Region, though on dates that did not clash with them. As well as being a keen rambler, George was a railway enthusiast and initially ran his excursions in association with organisations such as the Railway Enthusiasts Club and the Stephenson Locomotive Society, making them available to ramblers to fill up the seats.

His special trains would call first at a couple of destinations for the ramblers, then continue to run on little used lines, or even ones that had been closed to regular passenger traffic, and often included a visit to a train depot. Some of the excursions featured a literary or historical element, including a visit to a place associated with such worthies as George Bernard Shaw, William Penn and John Milton. However, it proved difficult to satisfy all elements of the clientèle and, though George continued to provide extensions that would appeal to railway enthusists, eventually the railway societies dropped out of the joint operation.

Some of George Lockie's excursions started at suburban stations and avoided central London e.g Greenford to Westerham, Greenford to Ardingly, Clapham Junction to Ongar and Crystal Palace to Chesham (though Michael Kohn has suggested that this could have gone via Sydenham, New Cross Gate, the East London Line under the Thames, Aldgate East and Baker Street).

The trains were given catchy names such as 'The West Meon Meteor', 'The Kentish Heights Special', 'The Essex Wealdman', 'The Kent & East Sussex Special' and 'The North Hampshire Downsman', and the steam locomotives that hauled them sported the appropriate headboard. A number of photographs appeared in the *The Railway Magazine* and *Trains Illustrated* at that time featuring locomotives hauling these excursions, and further information can be found on the website *www.sixbellsjunction.co.uk*.

In 1961 and 1962 George Lockie's excursions ran exclusively on the Eastern Region, still in his trademark style with the interests of railway enthusiasts at heart, though some were on the same dates as the coaches. One such trip, on Good Friday 1962, went to Ardleigh, Manningtree and Bentley on the Essex/Suffolk border for the ramblers, and linked with a special train consisting entirely of soon-to-be-scrapped brake vans running along the branch line to Hadleigh, which had been closed to passenger traffic in 1932 and was now maintained for freight only. One of the railway enthusiasts on this trip was a young lad called **Les Douglas**, who was to become in due course a rambling enthusiast, a leader, an organiser of ramble programmes, progenitor of the Commando Footpath Clearance Group and joint editor of *South Eastern Rambler* (now called *South East Walker*).

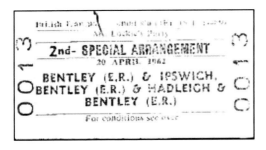

Les Douglas's ticket to ride a whole train of guard's vans.

A note on the Six Bells Junction website indicates that George Lockie organised his last excursion for ramblers and railway enthusiasts on 20 April 1962, after which he went to live in Spain. He later moved to the Isle of Man, where he died in January 1988.

The contribution that George Platt had made to the Southern excursions was realised when it came to replacing him as their organiser in 1983. Nobody could spare the amount of time he had spent, and it was necessary to replace him with four people: **Barry King** (Managing Director of the Tillingbourne Bus Company) as overall organiser for the Southern Region excursions, assisted by three divisional organisers (who were also regular leaders): **John Saunders** (South Western), **Gordon Bryant** (South Eastern) and **Michael Kohn** (South Central, known to everyone as Micky).

However, Barry King only served one year as overall co-ordinator, and from 1984 to 1993 Micky added the role of overall co-ordinator of all train and coach excursions to his existing South Central duties. He joined the RA Southern Area's Transport & Publicity Sub-Committee at its inception in 1974 and by the time it was wound up in 2004 (having become the Inner London Area's Transport Committee) he and Geoffrey Stevenson were the only two members who had served for all its 30 years' existence.

Gordon Bryant and Micky Kohn remained with their respective regions for many years: Gordon with South East until 2002 (when David Horwill took over) and Micky with South Central until the very end. After John Saunders stepped down from the South West region in 1985, **Brian Reader** then **Frank Busby** filled the gap for a while until 1989 when **Arthur Reed** came in to hold the reins until the end. In 1993 **Brenda and David Horwill** took over as joint overall co-ordinators until the end in 2004, allowing Micky to concentrate on South Central again.

North of the Thames, from 1954 until the early 1960s **Bob Mulholland** organised the Western Region excursions while George Lockie organised the Eastern Region ones in the early 1960s. Subsequently the Western, Midland and Eastern Regions were the responsibility of one organiser, and were known as the 'Other Regions' excursions.

From 1963 they were organised by **Arthur Hack,** for a while jointly with **Howard Gutteridge,** known as Gus (and incidentally an announcer at Waterloo Station – his dulcet tones were often heard as ramblers gathered on the concourse). Arthur Hack was born in Upper Holloway, London, on 22 August 1921. He was a very able

Gordon Bryant, organiser of the South Eastern excursions, on a hot day!

and enthusiastic organiser and is fondly remembered by excursionists, but sadly in 1973 he became very ill from cancer and was assisted by Graham Collett and Geoffrey Stevenson. Miffed by George Platt's antagonistic attitude to the excursion to Edale in November of that year, as described earlier, Arthur was delighted when Geoffrey visited him in hospital with the good news that it had gone very well, and died happy shortly afterwards, on 15 November at the early age of 52.

The 'Other Regions' then virtually became an enterprise of the Vanguards Rambling Club for the next 11 years, with the majority of organisers and leaders from among its ranks: from 1973 to 1975 **Graham Collett** assisted by **Andrew Ward**, then Andrew took over with assistance from **Graham Butler**; from 1977 **Gill Reader**, often acting jointly with husband **Brian Reader**, who from 1981 on the birth of their first son acted as sole organiser. In 1986 **Ron Jones** took over for a year, followed by **Clive Jones** (no relation, and neither of them Vanguards) until 1993, when **Geoffrey Stevenson** (who by then had been 'absorbed' into the Vanguards) stepped into the breach as described earlier.

'Other Regions' organisers Howard (Gus) Gutteridge and Arthur Hack.

Another well remembered organiser, though not actually of ramble excursions as such, was **Percy Danks**, who created the Merry-Maker rail trips (see page 33) that were much used by the 'Other Regions' excursions during the 1970s and early 1980s.

For a full list of organisers see page 91.

Leaders and rearguards

We know of some 320 leaders and rearguards over the eight decades covered by the ramblers' excursions – for a list of names see page 91. Many of them served as both leaders and rearguards at various times, and several were also organisers.

Without doubt the most regular leader of all was John Grinsell, who seemed to be ever present on both trains and coaches, probably leading well over a thousand times until he retired in 1981. On the coaches he invariably led the shorter of the two parties, which usually ncluded a visit to a stately home or other place of interest. Latterly he let Harold Lawrence lead the party but broke off after lunch to lead a detachment on a shorter route to the tea-stop. His usual rearguards were Fred Jex or Reg Miller on the trains and either Frank Millar or Harold Lawrence on the coaches.

Men initially dominated the leaders and rearguards, but women gradually entered the picture. We believe that Louise Holford was early on the scene, but the first female leader we know of for sure was Penny Keller on a Southern excursion on 24 July 1960 to Southwater, West Grinstead and Partridge Green. There were also some female rearguards by that time, including Ethel Chipchase and a Miss Webb, and the husband-and-wife teams of Denis and Kathleen Hicks and Stan and Betty Robinson were also around by then. The first recorded all-female leader/rearguard team was Ethel Chipchase and Margaret Kelland on 10 December 1961 to Holmwood, Ockley & Capel and Warnham. Of the 320 or so leaders in our list, 95 (30%) are women.

As well as the Hickses and Robinsons, several other husband-and-wife teams regularly led parties, including: Angela and Brian Bellwood, Jim and Vera Breeze, Dave and Janis Crake, Reg and Rena Glasscock, Brenda and David Horwill, Reg and Joan Miller, Brian and Gill Reader, Arthur and Sheila Reed, and Molly and Nick Steiner. The Breezes led something like 250 times between 1967 and 1992. *(Also see page 87 for the chapter on 'Romance'.)*

By the time the excursions were declining in the 1970s, it was becoming harder to find enough leaders and rearguards. Some help came from RA local groups, who were often willing to provide a leader when the excursions headed in their direction. One such was Paul Frances, who had been a regular on the excursions and after he moved to Berkshire continued to lead when the excursions went that way.

In 1987 the Transport Committee produced a set of 'Guidelines for Leaders of Rambles' – see inside back cover.

Micky Kohn confidently leads Party Number 2 away from the lunch pub at Datchworth Green, on the train ramble to Hertford North and Watton-at-Stone on 13 March 1983.
Shadowing him closely are fellow leaders Brian Reader and Sheila Reed.

The Clubs

At some point in their history, the train excursions started to be used by rambling clubs, and on the Southern Region special trains they could reserve compartments for their exclusive use by arrangement with the organiser. Their members were free to join the organised parties, and were likely to patronise a party led by one of their own. Sometimes they 'did their own thing', in which case, being smaller than the organised parties, they were able to start almost as soon as the train arrived and get away from the crowd of walkers clamouring around the official leaders.

The clubs that used the Southern excursions included:

Chums Rambling Club. Sadly, this no longer exists and we have little information. However, it is known that George Platt was closely linked with them and became their chairman after stepping down as Southern Region excursions organiser in 1982.

Connoisseur Rambling Club (popularly known as 'the Cons') was founded by Hugh E. Page in 1926, is still going strong and has put on a

Sunday walk throughout its entire existence. Other members who regularly joined the excursions included Arthur Hack, who organised the 'Other Regions' excursions for many years, Freddie Fear, a popular leader on the train rambles, the club's rambles organiser, Joan Brown, and Joyce Coles, who worked with author Colin Saunders at Waymark Holidays. Their website is *www.connoisseurramblers.btck.co.uk*.

Grinsell's Rambling Club has already been mentioned in several places.

Morley College Rambling Club was founded in 1912 and is now known simply as Morley Ramblers. They made frequent use of the train rambles, reserving two eight-person compartments and organising their own private walks. A gentleman called Walling Bryant was their rambles organiser from 1990 to 1998 and a regular leader for the club. Their website is *www.morleyramblers.co.uk*.

Polytechnic Rambling Club is one of the oldest walking clubs in the country, founded in 1885 (as a social club of the then Regent Street Polytechnic, now the University of Westminster). They now call themselves the Polyramblers, and their website is *www.blackcygnus.eu*.

Vanguards Rambling Club (see page 78).

Local Groups of the Ramblers' Association also took advantage of the special trains and included them in their programmes, especially:

West London Ramblers, established in 1955, whose members played a substantial role in organising and leading on the excursions, especially in the 1950s and 60s. For many years Bob Mulholland organised and led on the Western Region ones, and Arthur Hack (also of the 'Cons') on the 'Other Regions'. Other regular leaders and rearguards included Tom Berry, Ernie Lucas, Alan Payne, Carl Roe, Ken Royce and Ken Thornton, as well as several others who led private rambles for the group on the excursions. Their website is *www.westlondonramblers.org.uk*.

Kingston Ramblers – no doubt encouraged by their founding chairman from 1964, a certain George Platt! It appears that, for a while, he may have reduced the advertised fares by 6 old pence for their members. Their website is *www.kingston-ramblers.org.uk*.

Publicity and Promotion

Initially the excursions were promoted by means of handbills (see inside front cover) published and paid for by the train operators. As well as being available in leaflet racks at stations and enquiry offices, handbills were pinned to notice boards at places such as accommodation hostels for London store workers, and for a while this resulted in a considerable number of young foreigners attending the excursions during the late 1960s and early 1970s.

Until 1974 the handbills were supported by large (40 x 50 inches 'quad royal') posters displayed at stations and enquiry offices – some are held by the 'Search Engine', the library and archive of the National Railway Museum in York. At about this time, the handbills were redesigned and updated by David Sharp.

From its inception in 1970, *South Eastern Rambler* (later *South East Walker*, the RA's thrice-yearly magazine for members in most of its areas in South East England) published brief details of all the ramble excursions, and occasionally included features about them.

When rail operators stopped publishing handbills for the ramble excursions in 1983, the Transport Committee decided to publish a free quarterly newsletter, called *Sunday Rambler*, providing detailed information about forthcoming excursions over the next few months. Initially it was distributed on the excursions, and for a while it was stocked by the famous map shop, Stanfords of Long Acre.

The first editor was Les Douglas, then in 1987 Colin Saunders took over and changed the title to *London Rambler*. Later editors were Roger Wilsher, Liz Carr, Ronnie and Ann McArthur and Terry Davidson (with material written by David Horwill).

A free mailing list was started, but latterly a subscription was charged to cover postage, with subscriptions and mailing list administered by Sid and Sheila Stace. Distribution was a sizeable job, and several people mucked in with 'stuffing sessions' at Bridget Harper's flat in Earls Court.

As a result of the increasing number of phone calls to organisers' home numbers, in September 1988 the Transport Committee set up a Rambles Hotline to provide details of the forthcoming weekend's ramble excursion. It was operated by Colin Saunders until 1992 then by Bridget Harper until the end in 2004. The hotline was very well received and much used: on one occasion, a British Rail staff member even called it from New York to establish the following weekend's details and duly turned up as planned.

Occasionally free publicity was generated through editorial items, such as in an issue of *Coming Events in Britain* describing the train ramble to Haslemere and Liphook on 13 October 1968. In the 1980s, London Area's Publicity Committee had some success getting features on ramble excursions in several London regional publications including *Capital Commuter, On the Move* and *Oracle*. And in January 1985, an extensive feature appeared in the Mail on Sunday's supplement, *You*, following attendance on a train excursion to Merstham and Redhill by the Mail's resident astrologer, Sally Brompton. It took place in a snowstorm, and the party she joined, led by Ethel Chipchase, was described as 'an intrepid little band'.

During the 1990s there was some publicity for the excursions on Teletext and *Countrygoer* magazine, and on the Ramblers' Association websites (national and Inner London Area).

In 1994 a reciprocal publicity arrangement was made with NSE Railsport, which had been set up by Ron Glister of Network Southeast. He organised monthly Sunday rambles that were intended primarily for NSE staff, but in practice members of the public were free to join.

On the train ramble to Stansted Mountfitchet and Elsenham in August 1998, a Japanese journalist was investigating what British people did for recreation and spoke to Stanley Miller. Many months later the journalist sent Stanley the book she had written, all in Japanese, which also had a photo of him crossing a field.

During 2001-2002 excursions by train were listed in the Notice Board feature in *Country Walking* magazine and on their website.

Until *Sunday Rambler* started, there had been little promotion of the Ramblers' Association on the excursion literature, and for all their existence there was never much pressure on participants to join the RA, in fact it was stated that it was not necessary to be a member to go on the excursions. However, Geoffrey Stevenson took it upon himself to hand out RA leaflets on both train and coach excursions. *Sunday Rambler* and *London Rambler* included details of membership fees and benefits, but it seems likely that most excursionists were non-members.

6: OFFSHOOTS

The Vanguards Rambling Club

On the excursion to Axminster and Seaton on Easter Sunday 18 April 1965, a dozen or so young people who had been rambling together on this and several previous excursions could not find enough space in any one compartment to sit together on the homeward journey, so they piled into the guard's van. Someone produced a bottle of Drambuie to share, and amid the resulting bonhomie it was decided to get together the following day (Easter Monday) for a ramble in Richmond Park, when it was decided to call themselves, of course, the Vanguards.

Sometimes the Vanguards would start out with an organised party, then stay on at the pub and find their own way back. But they often went their own way, deciding that the organised parties 'weren't tough enough'. In their early days, it was not unusual for them to walk up to 20 miles including a longer than usual stop at the lunch pub.

Fellow excursionists at this time would have been amazed to learn that this unruly and noisy mob, whose homeward journey largely consisted of the raucous singing of rugby songs and other shenanigans, would eventually produce many leaders, rearguards and even organisers for future excursions.

Many members have become Ramblers' Association activists: at one time about 25 sat on the 100-strong Council of the old Southern Area, and nine have been members of the Inner London Group's Transport Committee. They have provided an RA national chairman (Brian Reader), a president of Essex Area (John Jenkins) and officers for the Inner London, Surrey and Norfolk Areas. One RA luminary, with tongue firmly in cheek, was prompted to describe the Vanguards as 'the Mafia of the Ramblers' Association'!

Some 50 Vanguards became leaders or rearguards on both trains and coaches. The first to lead a party was Peter Willis on 14 November 1965, subsequently with, as his rearguard, Bill Ramsey, who went on to lead many times himself. Micky Kohn and Brian Reader became organisers on the Southern excursions, while Graham Butler, Graham Collett, Brian Reader, Gill Reader and Andrew Ward took turns at organising the Other Regions. Even Geoffrey Stevenson eventually became a Vanguard.

Vanguards were instrumental in setting up and organising the Commandos (see below), and setting up and leading the Saturday Strolls, now a key element in the programme of the London Strollers Group of The Ramblers.

In due course many Vanguards had to reduce their attendance on the excursions due to family and other commitments, but some supported the excursions to the very end, continuing on to Geoff's Jaunts, and now (approaching their Golden Jubilee) they organise their own programme of walks and social events.

The club has developed its own long distance trail, the **Vanguard Way**, which runs for 66 miles from Croydon to Newhaven. Its website is *www.vanguardway.org.uk*.

The Commandos
Not the paramilitary wing of the Ramblers but the Commando Footpath Clearance Group. Although officially an initiative of the erstwhile Southern Area of the Ramblers' Association, it was very closely associated with the ramblers' excursions in practice as most

of its organisers and members were Vanguards and other regular excursionists. During their 27-year existence, according to surviving records, the Commandos tackled nearly 150 clearances and made a substantial contribution to the maintenance of many miles of footpaths in south-east England.

The clearances took place in all the counties of the RA's old Southern Area: Essex (21), Surrey (20), Oxon (20), Kent (16), Bucks (13), Herts (10), Greater London (9), Beds (8), East Sussex (6), Hants (6), Suffolk (4), Berks (3), West Sussex (2), Norfolk (2), Dorset (1), plus 3 for which the locations are as yet unknown.

In November 1969, Les Douglas, a ramblers excursions leader and a Vanguard, wrote to Vic Morecroft, Secretary of the Southern Area, to suggest that the Area should set up a team of volunteers who would be willing to travel to any part of the south-east and help with major footpath clearances that local groups felt were too big to tackle by themselves. It was agreed that the team should be called the Commando Footpath Clearance Group, and the task of organising it was taken on first by Graham Collett, later Joe Welsh, John Jenkins, Les Douglas, David Norfolk, Paul Miall, Eric Sanders and Ken Blake, with assistance from Graham Butler, Ian Mitchell and Colin Saunders.

A sizeable collection of tools was amassed over the years and stored by various people including David Rogerson and Ian Mitchell. They included a variety of saws, loppers (always for some reason called 'toggle-loppers' by the Commandos), sickles, weed-whips (always breaking), billhooks with short and long handles (the latter always called 'slashers'), and even a pitchfork. The slashers were quickly seized by some of the stronger male members, who then proceeded to slash away ahead of the main group, with the result that these particular tools often came to grief due to over-enthusiastic use.

Some 20 regular excursionists and other individuals (often supplemented by members of local organisations) were signed up, largely on the premise that they would "be working in healthy open air, roasting chestnuts and baking potatoes around an open fire, picking blackberries and visiting quaint old country inns at lunchtime". What they often found, though, was that their clothing could be torn to ribbons by blackthorn, brambles and barbed wire, they would be knee-deep in mud, the wood was too wet to burn, the only berries were haws or sloes and the nearest pub was miles away.

Yet, in spite of these hardships, the Group generally managed to enjoy themselves, and it must be admitted that they were usually more productive in the morning session, less so after the lunchtime pub! With the exception of Ken Blake, who steadfastly refused to visit the pub and worked all day, guarding the fire while everyone else sank a pint or two.

Normally, clearances took place on Saturdays once a month in autumn and winter, but none during the nesting and holiday periods. The first clearance was at East Hoathly, East Sussex, in September 1970, and (with the exception of the 1984-85 season) the group was kept steadily occupied until 1997, with encouragement from local authorities, some of whom even offered to pay the group's travelling expenses.

Some clearances required two days (the second day sometimes at another nearby site), camping overnight on site or staying at a convenient youth hostel. On one occasion when camping, the local landowner and his wife rode out on horseback and threw bags of apples at the breakfasting Commandos – presumably as largesse in appreciation of their hard work! Another, less pleasant, encounter involved a heated verbal altercation with the daughter of a tenant farmer, who had not been informed by the landowner that the team had his permission.

The return journey from the clearance at Weybourne in Norfolk over the weekend of 19-20 August 1972 was notable for Frank Barker, Ian Mitchell and Colin Saunders missing the connecting train at Norwich after being dispatched to buy cans of beer at an off-licence near the station. It was the last train to London, and their rucksacks were on it! Colin worked for Trusthouse Forte at the time and was able to arrange a meal and accommodation at the local Post House, then they returned to London on the Monday morning.

Over the weekend of 18-19 October 1980 the Commandos celebrated their 10th anniversary with dinner, bed and breakfast at the Boship Farm Hotel near Hailsham, East Sussex.

Had they been operating now, the Commandos would have been required to take out insurance, so they were very fortunate that, without it, no major incidents occurred. Though once in Essex the fire brigade was called out by a neighbour who thought that the brushwood fire was out of control, but in fact was in capable hands. Another time, one Commando's finger was slashed by a billhook that was being brandished by another, and had to be patched up at a nearby hospital.

The Commandos were fully employed until the early 1980s, but the break-up of the vast Southern Area in October 1984 led to the establishment of more locally focussed areas and groups, which became capable of tackling clearance work without outside help. The 1984-85 season saw the Commandos unemployed and in danger of folding, but from 1985-86 they were found work by a variety of non-RA groups including the Chiltern Society, the Trustees of Monken Hadley Common, near Barnet, and the Wey & Arun Canal Trust (to clear the towpath).

Indeed, the Commandos took on a new lease of life. The clearance at Albury, Surrey, in February 1988 was graced by the attendance of a reporter and photographer for a two-page spread in the Sunday Telegraph's magazine section, while Radio Oxford brought their roving reporter car to the one at Bletchington, Oxon, in February 1991 to interview RA organiser Jo Bird and some of the Commandos. Articles often appeared in local newspapers, though one featured a photograph of an inebriated rambler who happened to pick up a pair of toggle-loppers while staggering through!

The rejuvenated Commandos found plenty of work for several more years, but by the late 1990s demand for their services had fizzled out, with Ken Blake, Colin Hills, Geoffrey Stevenson and a handful of others occasionally helping informally with small tasks at Monken Hadley and on the Wey & Arun.

Appendix B (see page 2) provides dates and locations of the Commandos' work.

Yuletide Rambles

For many years Geoffrey Stevenson, never one to be deprived of a ramble, put together his own programme on perhaps half a dozen days during the Christmas/New Year period, using the London Underground and suburban rail services, and visiting parks and open spaces within Greater London such as Hampstead Heath and Richmond Park. They were well attended and gave Geoff an opportunity to take his friends to his favourite watering holes.

Saturday Strolls and Waterside Walks

Though not directly resulting from the ramblers' excursions, in 1987 two programmes were set up by the Transport Committee, which were organised and led by Vanguards. They were the Saturday Afternoon Strolls (later Saturday Strolls), originally organised and led by Angela Ferrari (later Bellwood), then Colin Saunders and later Les Douglas, and the Wednesday Evening Canal Walks (later called Waterside Walks) originally organised and led by Les Douglas and later Mike Biggs.

For a while the Saturday Strolls were sponsored by LBC Radio, who broadcast details and paid for publicity material. The Canal Walks were briefly supported by British Waterways; on one occasion, when the walk started at Bethnal Green and finished at Camden Lock, they even provided a waterbus to transport participants to Little Venice – an attraction that drew 214 walkers to the event.

These events continue to the present day, now part of the programme of the London Strollers group of The Ramblers.

Grinsell's Christmas Holidays

For over 50 years, from before the Second World War, under the auspices of Grinsell's Rambling Club, Len King organised 5/6-day

Christmas holidays on behalf of Grinsell's Rambling Club (though many of his other excursionist friends went too), usually staying at either the Nelson Hotel in Norwich or the Grand Hotel in Bristol. Len went to a great deal of trouble to ensure that everything was right: he and Annette (often accompanied by Cyril Freeman) visited the area the previous September to check the hotel arrangements and find out what would be open over the Christmas period.

Participants would attend midnight mass on Christmas Eve, have the traditional Christmas lunch on Christmas Day, watch a pantomime on Boxing Day, and on the following evening the hotel sometimes provided a dinner-dance for all guests. There were rambles each day, led by John Grinsell until he died in 1986, then by Geoffrey Stevenson, and something was laid on as well for non-ramblers.

When Len died in 1999 Annette organised the tour, then Cyril the following one, after which the Grinsell's people joined up with trips organised by Judith Whitworth for all the subsequent Christmas holidays until 2010.

Geoff's Jaunts

Dear Geoffrey Stevenson: Rambler Supreme, and an excursionist to the last! After the official excursions programme came to an end in 2004 he continued on his own initiative to organise informal fortnightly outings by train, which became popularly known as 'Geoff's Jaunts' and were similar in style to the official ones, though usually somewhat shorter and with just one party.

After falling terminally ill in 2010 he passed the reins to John McGahern and Roger Kemp, who at the time of writing continue to organise such trips, still under the banner of 'Geoff's Jaunts' in his memory. As well as Geoffrey, John and Roger, leaders and rearguards have included Mike Biggs, Sue Clark, Keith Evans, Paul Frances, Bridget Harper, Michael Jenkins, David Laws, Stan Miller, Elizabeth Shaw, Mike Stabler and Andrew Ward.

For further details of Geoff's Jaunts contact Roger Kemp – see page 142.

7. MISCELLANEA

Public Holidays and Special Excursions

In pre-war years, rambler's excursions took place on five public holidays: Good Friday, Easter Monday, Whit Monday, August Bank Holiday and Boxing Day. After the war, it took a while for such days to be considered suitable for an excursion and until 1967 this happened no more than once a year, either on Good Friday or August Bank Holiday, though not every year. But from 1968 excursions ran every Good Friday and August Bank Holiday, and they were augmented within a few years on Easter Monday and Whit Monday (or Late May Bank Holiday as it became known), and from 1978 by the new Mayday or Spring Bank Holiday. The most regrettable decision in the early 1960s to stop operating trains on Boxing Day put this option out of reach. There was occasionally an excursion on either New Year's Eve or New Year's Day.

Because of the strange congestion of public holidays in England in the Spring, when Easter fell late in some years there was the anomaly of four extra excursions within a five week period.

There were six special extra bank holidays, and advantage was taken of all of them for a ramblers' excursion: Monday 6 May 1935 (King George V Silver Jubilee), Wednesday 12 May 1937 (King George VI Coronation), Tuesday 2 June 1953 (Queen Elizabeth II Coronation), Tuesday 7 June 1977 (Queen Elizabeth II Silver Jubilee), Monday 3 January 2000 (Millennium) and Monday 3 June 2002 (Queen Elizabeth II Golden Jubilee).

Although no official excursion took place on the special public holiday on Wednesday 29 July 1981, when Prince Charles married Lady Diana Spencer, Geoffrey Stevenson was not to be denied the opportunity of a good walk and organised an unofficial one anyway.

Three special extra excursions were organised on Saturdays: on 11 April 1987 to Taunton and Minehead jointly with the West Somerset Railway Society; on 26 September 1987 to celebrate the electrification of the Sanderstead-East Grinstead line, and on 1 October 1988 to celebrate the centenary of the Oxted-Uckfield line.

Dancing and Reunions

Perhaps bizarrely, some of the pre-war excursions included dancing – not during the rambles but afterwards! This was the era of the great dance bands when halls throughout the country offered tea and supper dances almost daily.

On Guy Fawkes Night, Saturday 5 November 1932, an excursion to Brighton started with a Chinese lantern procession up to Devil's Dyke for a bonfire there, after which the ramblers attended a dinner-dance in Brighton and continued on to a ramble on the following day. A similar excursion took place the following New Year's Eve.

On 7 April (Rickmansworth) and 18 August 1935 (St Albans) the LMS Sunday excursions included a tea-dance with Stan Atkin's Recording Band. Southern followed with tea-dances on their trips to Maidstone on 31 October 1936 and 6 March 1937, when a cream tea and late refreshments were provided and, according to the handbill, "the dancing will take place in a magnificent hall with sprung floor". In case anyone was tempted to dance in their walking boots, ramblers were advised that dancing shoes were essential! A moonlight ramble was offered to non-dancers. The return trains on these excursions left for London at about 9 pm.

Hugh E. Page also organised some well attended 'Southern Region Ramblers' Reunion Dances' at central London venues on winter evenings between 1934 and 1939.

Post-war, we know of no ramblers' excursion that included dancing, but reunion dances took place occasionally: we have records of events on 22 September 1957 and 4 April 1959 (both at the Conway Hall in Red Lion Square, WC1) one at the Abbey Community Centre in Marsham Street, SW1, on 31 October 1959, and another on 11 February 1961 (venue not known). There were also reunions with no dancing at the Royal Festival Hall – we know of one on 14 February 1959.

More recently, regular reunions of former excursionists (and current Geoff's Jaunters) have been taking place at the Railway Hotel in

Putney, which all former excursionists are welcome to attend. For details contact Roger Kemp – see page 142.

Map Reading Courses

In 1987 the Transport Committee decided to try a series of free map reading courses with the aim of encouraging new faces to the leader panel. Organised by Micky Kohn and Pat Hobbs, they took place on selected train excursions and were limited to five participants. Unfortunately they were not well supported and came to an end after a few years.

Romance

Many people go rambling with groups in the hope of finding friendship and even romance. Many couples met on the excursions and later married, some even becoming leader/rearguard teams, including David Horwill and Brenda Allen, Arthur Reed and Sheila Best.

No fewer than fourteen Vanguard couples met or consolidated their relationship on the excursions, including Brian Bellwood and Angela Ferrari, Graham Butler and Janet Wells, Graham Collett and Hazel Kitley, Dave and Janis Crake, Steve Deverill and Pam Blades, Dave Dowsett and Sheila Webb, Bob Goodman and Beatriz Valladares, Mike Herniman and Tania Knapman, John Hobbs and Pat Baumgarten, Jim Kirk and Paula Hazelden, Graham Miller and Jenny Cooke, Robin Ray and Linda Harman, Brian Reader and Gill Allchin, David Wright and Linda Fuller.

Support for charities

Collections were made, usually on the homeward journey, on behalf of several charitable organisations, principally the Ramblers' Association, but also the National Trust or the Railwaymen's Homes at Woking.

On many occasions excursionists volunteered to act as companions for blind and partially sighted members of the London Sports Club for the Disabled.

Stations

Most of the stations that appear in Appendix A (see page 2) will be familiar to those who went on the train rambles, but sadly many of those visited in the early days, as well as the lines they occupied, have disappeared – lost mainly as a result of wartime depradations or the Beeching axe during the mid 1960s. Sounding like an excerpt from Flanders' and Swann's *Slow Train*, they include (with years of closure in brackets where known):

Alresford* (1973), Amesbury (1952), Ampthill (1959), Ardingly (1958), Ashwell (Rutland, 1948), Ayot (1948), Bakewell (1967), Barham (1940), Baynards (1965), Blake Hall (1994), Bodiam* (1954), Bordon (1966), Brackley (1966), Bramber (1966), Bramley & Wonersh (Surrey, 1965), Bramshot Halt (1946), Brasted (1961), Braughing (1964), Breamore (1964), Brentor (1968), Bridestowe (1968), Brimscombe (1964), Buntingford (1964), Burghclere (1960), Castlethorpe (1964), Chalford (1964), Charwelton (1963), Chiltern Green (1952), Claydon (1968), Combpyne (1965), Corfe Castle* (1972), Cranbrook (1961), Cranleigh (1965), Croxley Green (1996), Daggons Road (1964), Dinton (1966), Dorton Halt (1963), Droxford (1955), Dunmow (1961), Dunstable Town (1965), East Langton (1968), Elham (1940), Elsted (1955), Fittleworth (1955), Fordingbridge (1964), Forest Row (1967), Groombridge* (1985), Goudhurst (1961), Grange Road (1967), Hadham (1964), Harringworth (1948), Hartfield (1967), Hawkhurst (1961), Heathfield (1965), Henfield (1966), Highclere (1960), Holmsley (1964), Horsebridge (1964), Horsmonden (1961), Horsted Keynes* (1963), Hothfield (1959), Kibworth (1968), Kingscote* (1963), Kingsley Halt (1957), Litchfield (1960), Lyme Regis (1965), Lyminge (1947), Manton (1966), Marlborough (1961), Masbury (1966), Mayfield (1965), Medstead & Four Marks* (1973), Midhurst (1955), Mountfield Halt (1969), Napsbury (1959), Newton Toney (1952), Northiam* (1954), North Weald* (1994), Oakley (1963), Ongar* (1994), Padbury (1964), Partridge Green (1966), Petworth (1955), Privett (1955), Quainton Road* (1963), Redbourn (1947), Roade (1964), Rogate (1955), Ropley* (1973), Rotherfield (1965), Rowfant (1967),

Rudgwick (1965), Savernake (1966), Seaton Junction (1966), Selham (1955), Semley (1966), Sharnbrook (1960), Shepton Mallet (1966), Slinfold (1965), Smeeth (1954), Southwater (1966), Standon (1964), Steyning (1966), Stockbridge (1967), Sutton Scotney (1960), Swanage* (1972), Takeley (1952), Tenterden* (1954), Tisted (1955), Tunbridge Wells West* (1985), Ventnor (1966), Walton (Cambs, 1953), Wantage Road (1964), Weedon (1958), Westerham (1961), West Grinstead (1966), West Hoathly (1955), West Meon (1955), West Mill (1964), West Wycombe (1958), Wheathampstead (1965), Winchester Chesil (1961), Withyham (1967), Wroxall (1966).

These stations have subsequently reopened on heritage lines.

Some stations that appear in Appendix A are still open but may not be familiar as they have changed their names. They include (previous name or names with current name in brackets):
Amersham & Chesham Bois (Amersham)
Boxhill, or Boxhill & Burford Bridge (Boxhill & Westhumble)
Crowborough & Jarvis Brook (Crowborough)
Dorking North (Dorking Main)
Dorking Town (Dorking West)
Fawkham (Longfield)
Gomshall & Shere (Gomshall)
Hemel Hempstead & Boxmoor (Hemel Hempstead)
Lyghe Halt (Leigh Halt)
Malling (replaced by East and West Malling)
Ockley & Capel (Ockley)
Sevenoaks Tubs Hill (Sevenoaks)
Ticehurst Road (Stonegate)
Wrotham & Borough Green (Borough Green & Wrotham)

8. ROLL CALL
The following lists are taken from various sources including Transport Committee minutes, excursion itineraries, Commando News and other documents. Apologies to anyone omitted in error. If you were, or know somebody who was, involved as an organiser, leader or rearguard and not named here, please contact the pubisher.

A group of ramblers awaits the departure of their party from Liphook Station, possibly in the 1960s.

Transport Committee

The following were members at various times over its 30-year existence from inception in June 1974 to winding up in December 2004:

Angela (Ferrari) Bellwood, Brian Bellwood, Gordon Bryant,
Frank Busby, Graham Butler, Graham Collett, Bill Craies, Ted Cutter,
Terry Davidson, Les Douglas, Bridget Harper, Brenda (Allen) Horwill,
David Horwill, Clive Jones, Barry King, Michael Kohn,
Harold Lawrence, Ann McArthur, Ronnie McArthur, George Platt,
Brian Reader, Arthur Reed, Sheila Reed, Colin Saunders,
John Saunders, Geoffrey Stevenson, Roger Towle, Roger Wilsher.

Organisers

Gordon Bryant, Norman Burchill, Frank Busby, Graham Butler, Graham Collett, John Grinsell, Howard Gutteridge, Arthur Hack, Brenda Horwill, David Horwill, Clive Jones, Ron Jones, Barry King, Len King, Michael Kohn, George Lockie, Bob Mulholland, Hugh E. Page, George Platt, Brian Reader, Gill Reader, Arthur Reed, John Saunders, Geoffrey Stevenson, Andrew Ward.

Leaders and Rearguards

Francis Adkin, Kathleen Akass, Vic Alexander, David Allard, Roger Allen, Mrs Allen, Peter Armitage, Dave Ash, Alex Badenoch, Catherine Badenoch, Janis Badenoch, Will Bagley, Eddie Banks, Frank Barker, Cliff Barnes, John Barry, Magda Bauer, Brian Baxter, Hubert Beale, Angela (Ferrari) Bellwood, Brian Bellwood, Tom Benson, Jim Berra, Jennifer Berry, Tom Berry, Mr T. Bird, Tom Boniface, Richard Bonner, Rena Borg, Peter Bowden, Michael Bower-Meale, Jim Breeze, Vera Breeze, Bernard Broadway, Alan Brown, Jessica Brown, Joan Brown, John Brown, Gordon Bryant, Norman Burchill, Miss J. Burton, Frank Busby, Dave Bush, Mr G. Bushell, Graham Butler, Hugh Byford, Rosanna Cavallo, Stan Chase, Ethel Chipchase, Brenda Clarke, Joanna Clegg, Bernard Cload, Harry Coles, Graham Collett, Hazel Collett, Gerald Colton, Tim Constantine, Ted Cossor, Albert Cotton, Shirley Cotton, Mr R. Cox, Bill Craies, Dave Crake, Janis Crake, Jack Crisp, Alan Cushion, Ted Cutter, Vera Cutter, Alan Davidson, Vera Davidson, Gerald Davies, Jerry Delaney, Donald Dibben, Mr R. Dinsey, Sheila Doey, Les Douglas, Dave Dowsett, Audrey Dymond, Mr J. Eades, Millie East, Ray East, Michael Easter, Doug Edwards, Mr F. Eldridge Smith, Jim Elliott, Jane Emerson, Andy Evans, Keith Evans, Freddie Fear, Sam Fenn, Mr Ferguson, Dick Field, Bob Finch, Gretha Flanders, Tony Flanders, Gordon Ford, Paul Frances, Sally Frances, Donald Fraser, Brenda Fruin, Michael Fuller, Gerry Gale, Alan Gardner, Mr D.C.M. Gardner, Tom Gardner, Mr H. Garrath, Dave Garwood, Peter George, John Gilroy, Reg Glasscock, Rena Glasscock, Peter Goad, Beatriz Goodman, Bob Goodman, Don

Goodwin, Mr R. Gould, Linda Graham, Martin Green, Clive
Greenhill, Dave Griffin, Wendy Griffiths, John Grinsell, Anne Gurney,
Roger Gurtner, Howard Gutteridge, Arthur Hack, Audrey Hack,
Margaret Hadfield, Jenny Hale, Ken Hall, Dorothy Hardy, Richard
Hare, May Harlock, Ron Harmer, Bridget Harper, Bill Harris,
Christopher Harrison, Mr G. Hawker, Freddie Hearn, Mrs B. Hearn,
Peter Hearn, George Helm, Mary Helm, Mr J. Hemmings, Albert
Henderson, Mike Herniman, Johanna Hickey, Denis Hicks, Kathleen
Hicks, Colin Hills, John Hodges, Louise Holford, Brenda (Allen)
Horwill, David Horwill, Bob Howard, Renata (Turcic) Howell,
Horace Huxley, Chris Jackson, Pauline James, Jean Jeffcoate, John
Jenkins, Fred Jex, Phyllis Jex, Howard Johnson, Bill Jones, Clive Jones,
David Jones, Ron Jones, Sid Kaufman, Sally Keeble, Margaret Kelland,
Penny Keller, Richard Kendall, Cara Kensit, Arthur Kent, Chris Kew,
J. Knight, Maurice Knights, Michael Kohn, Len Kottnitz, Dave Lamb,
Harold Lawrence, Marie Lawrence, Nat Lofthouse, Mr B. Lowd, Ernie
Lucas, Kay McClean, Tony McColm, John McGahern, Bernard Mabon,
Jan Macleod, Petre Mais, Barbara March, Stella Mariani, Lindsay
Marson, Walter Martin, Howard Mason, Alex Masson, Ian
Masterman, Fred Matthews, Angela May, Anne Maynard, Bob
Maynard, Joan Middleton, Michael Middleton, Alwyn Miles, Frank
Millar, Cecil Miller, Joan Miller, Pat Miller, Reg Miller, Stanley Miller,
Stuart Mills, Ian Mitchell, Margaret Moore, Basil Morley, Bob
Mulholland, Mrs Mulholland, Bob Munslow, Mr A.T. Nelson, Dave
Newcombe, Patricia Norris, Bob North, Conal O'Sullivan, Audrey
Osborne, John Osborne, Anne Ossowska, Alex Oxley, Hugh E. Page,
Robin Parker, Alan Payne, Andy Payne, Chris Pearce, Arthur Penn,
David Peters, Neal Pike, Bridget Platt, George Platt, Bob Pucknell, Mr
G.P. Quantrill, Bill Ramsey, Michael Read, Brian Reader, Gill (Allchin)
Reader, Pete Redwood, Arthur Reed, Sheila (Best) Reed, Barbara
Rice, Colin Richards, Pamela Richards, May Richardson, Keith Rix,
Betty Robinson, Stan Robinson, Carl Roe, Neville Rogers, David
Rogerson, John Rosser, Ken Royce, Alan Rubridge, Angela Salisbury,
George Sanderson, Mrs E. Sanderson, Pat Sansom, Colin Saunders,

John Saunders, Peter Saxton, Kaye Sears, David Secker, Lesley Secker, Robin Setchell, Edith Sharp, Mary Shepherdson, Norma Shirley, Cyril Simmonds, John Simmonds, Diane Slough, Leslie Smart, Alan Smith, Charles Smith, Derek Smith, Mr R.E. (Roe) Smith, Philip Solly, Barbara Spencer, Gordon Spencer, Michael Stabler, Molly Steiner, Nick Steiner, Geoffrey Stevenson, Mr H. Tanner, Dennis Taylor, Bill Thatcher, Ken Thornton, Ron Thwaites, Roger Towle, Hazel Tucker, Wendy Tucker, Peter Uren, Christine Varndell, Ken Varndell, Martin Vyne, Charles Wake, Alan Walkenden, Mr G.W. Wallington, Matthew Wallis, Andrew Ward, Bill Watkins, Bill Webb, Miss Webb, Gertrude Weil, Ivan Wheeler, Gladys White, John Whitehouse, Martin Wilkins, Peter Willis, Alan Withers, David Wright, Irene Wright, Linda (Fuller) Wright.

The Commandos

This list excludes members of Ramblers' Association local groups and other local organisations that participated jointly with the Commandos on some clearances.

Francis Adkin, Barbara Allchin, Bill Baker, Frank Barker, Sue Bellamy, Angela Ferrari, Ken Blake, Graham Butler, Janet Butler, Robin Carr, Pete Clegg, Ken Cole, Graham Collett, Jack Crisp, Rosemary Davern, Les Douglas, David Dowsett, Linda Fuller, Delia Haldane, Bridget Harper, Colin Hills, Malcolm Jackson, Pauline James, John Jenkins, Arthur Kent, Chris Kew, Hazel Kitley, Michael Kohn, David Lamb, Trevor Liddle, Alan Mattingly, Chris Meeks, Paul Miall, Joan Middleton, Michael Middleton, Geoffrey Mitchell, Ian Mitchell, Bob Munslow, David Norfolk, Michael Pender, Bill Ramsey, Lynn Ray, Robin Ray, Brian Reader, Gill (Allchin) Reader, Keith Rix, David Rogerson, Joe Salmon, Eric Sanders, Colin Saunders, Andrew Scarf, Joe Scarf, Edith Sharp, Alan Smith, Mike Stenning, Geoffrey Stevenson, Jack Taylor, Ruth Tucker, Andrew Ward, Sheila Webb, Joe Welsh, David Wright.

Do not approach this man!

The author getting a little carried away in charge of tools on a Commando Clearance (Wey & Arun Canal Towpath, January 1995).

10. TIMELINE

All dates are Sundays unless shown otherwise.

<u>1932</u>
March 25: Great Western Railways 'Hikers' Mystery Express No.1' to Tilehurst and Pangbourne. Among its passengers are Messrs H.E. Page and S.P.B. Mais, who conceive the idea of ramblers' excursion trains on Southern Railway.
May 15: First Southern Railway ramblers excursion by special train to Kingscote and West Hoathly, organised by Mr H.E. Page.

<u>1935</u>
August 4-5: First Southern Railway ramblers' excursion to France (Dieppe via Newhaven).

1939

August 20: Last ramble excursions to operate before the Second World War, to Bentley and Bordon (organised by Hugh E. Page) and Rickmansworth (organised by John Grinsell).

August 27 onwards: Scheduled excursions cancelled due to fears of impending war with Germany (which was declared on September 3).

August 1939 to March 1949

Ramble excursions suspended during and immediately after the Second World War. Hugh E. Page and John Grinsell maintain rambling activities every Sunday with their respective Connoisseur and Grinsell's Rambling Clubs, despite much of the countryside being in restricted military zones and with limited public transport.

1949

April 3: First train ramble excursion since the Second World War to Pulborough and Amberley, organised by Huge E. Page.

April 10: George Platt leads his first party on train ramble excursion to Gomshall, Chilworth, Shalford.

1951

October 21: Train ramble excursion cancelled due to fuel crisis.

October 1951 to June 1952

Train ramble excursions suspended due to fuel crisis. Hugh E. Page decides to step down as organiser, hands over to George Platt.

1952

June 2: First train ramble excursion since suspension, to Haslemere and Liphook. George Platt's first excursion as organiser.

1954

October 10: First excursion believed to have been organised by George Lockie for both ramblers and railway enthusiasts, to Berkhamsted and Tring.

1955

April 8 (Good Friday): 21-year old Geoffrey Stevenson attends his first ramble excursion, by train to Henley-on-Thames.

1955 continued

October 1: First ramble excursion by coach to Nettlebed and Henley, organised by Len King and Norman Burchill, with parties led by John Grinsell and Hugh E. Page.

1958

May 4: 1,200 ramblers turn up for excursion to Isle of Wight on special train with only 700 seats. George Platt organises extra capacity on trains and ferries for overflow.

1959

August: Hugh E.Page killed in road accident while surveying for excursion to the Chilterns.

1965

April 18: Vanguards Rambling Club established following train ramble to Axminster and Seaton, when they occupied the guard's van on the return journey.

1966

Geoffrey Stevenson takes over from Norman Burchill as joint organiser with Len King of coach excursions.

November 1967 to January 1968

Rambles affected by outbreak of foot-and-mouth disease.

1971

May 31: First Merry-Maker excursion to be used for an official rambler's excursion, to Matlock.

1973

15 November: Arthur Hack dies.

1974

September 15: Last ramblers' special excursion train, to Cooksbridge, Lewes and Glynde. From now on all excursions used scheduled service trains.

1982

December 12: George Platt's last excursion as organiser.

1986
May 3: John Grinsell dies.

1987
October 15-16: The 'Great Storm' adversely affects ramblers throughout southern England.

1998
February 27: George Platt dies.

1999
May 29: Len King dies.

2000
December 10: The final ramblers' excursion by coach from London, to Whipsnade, Kensworth, Caddington and Stockwood Park.

2001
February to July: All rambles affected by another outbreak of foot-and-mouth disease.

2004
December 18: The final ramblers' excursion by train from London, to Chelsfield.

2010
July 16: Geoffrey Stevenson dies.

PART 2: REMINISCING

This section consists of the very special memories that many former ramblers' excursionists have kindly contributed to this story. They are shown in five groups:

Date-specific memories – those for which we know the date, shown in chronological order.

Undated memories – those for which we have no date and are shared by a number of former excursionists, so have not been ascribed to any particular person.

Personal memories – those from individuals for which we have no date.

Geoff o'Stick memories – there are so many about Geoffrey that this group is devoted entirely to him.

Geoff's Jaunts – amusing incidents continue to arise on the successor to the official excursions.

However, we start with a very special reminiscence by **Rosalie Saunders**, mother of well known long distance walker Jill Green (but no relation of the author). It is the only recollection we have of the early ramblers' excursions in the 1930s. As Rosalie Hill, she started walking with the Croydon CHA Rambling Club in 1937, when she was 20, and died in 1997 at the age of 91. The following reminiscence is based on a talk that Rosalie gave at the 75th anniversary of the Croydon CHA Rambling Club in 1996, when she was the longest-serving member aged 80, and recalls the conditions in which rambling took place at that time:

> How different it was. You had to get to the starting place by train, as none of us had cars. There were ramblers' excursion trains, run by the railways to the more out of the way stations, which were very well patronised: just one train out in the morning and one back. My first one went to Hever and several stations beyond, and I remember we had to run the last three miles to reach the station in time for the homeward train. We worked out our own routes then.

Rosalie Saunders strides out with the Croydon CHA
Rambling Club on an excursion in the 1930s.

Then equipment – plastic hadn't been invented, nor commando soles etc, so we bought boys' boots and hammered those three-pronged studs into the soles to give a grip. Often the heels weren't up to the job and came off. Waterproofs were either that yellow oiled silk and weighed a ton, or else rubberised macintoshes which tended to perish and stink of rotten rubber. They let water in all the creases. I used to wear a brown macintosh cape, and when you jumped off a stile it was like a parachute!

No trousers or slacks for women, and nylon hadn't been invented so it was all heavy. I had a hand-knitted woollen skirt which got bigger every time it rained, so the hem was turned over as the years went by. It was so thick it rubbed the backs of my calves raw. We wore stockings with seams (no tights yet) and woollen ankle socks to help fill up the boys' boots and stop blisters. Shoes weren't much good because they tended to come off in the mud and get full of water. Crocheted woolly hats kept out the wind (pre-balaclava of course) and the rain-hat was a sou'wester, tied under the chin (no anoraks with hoods then). We wore jumpers or an aertex short-sleeved blouse. Skirts were mid-calf length or thereabouts and shorts were unheard of for rambling. Though I believe the so-called hikers did perhaps wear them – but hikers were the younger, louder sort of people, and we were definitely ramblers, not hikers! The older women (i.e those aged 35+) often wore hats on rambles but I never did, and the men often wore jackets and ties.

Most people worked a five-and-a-half-day week, so on Saturdays we weren't available until midday. We ate a sandwich lunch en route, then walked to the tea-place. After tea, we would walk a further five or six miles to the station to get the mileage in, often in the dark, so it was advisable to carry a torch for rutted fields. On Sundays we took a packed lunch to eat in a field, or a barn if you were lucky. The leader had to find a tea-place to book in advance – these usually accommodated the party at trestle tables, with a huge teapot and lashings of bread, butter and jam, and it cost about a shilling for as much as you cared to eat.

One of our leaders, John Saunders (whom I married in 1940!), had a pencil that he used for working out walks on the maps. The length of the pencil (about six-and-a-half inches) gave him an area in which to look for shelter for lunchtime sandwiches, then a further pencil-length gave him the area to search for a tea-place, and a final pencil-length got us to the homeward station.

We were lucky with trains in that your ticket to one station would be equally valid for the return journey from a different station on a different line, with no questions asked – a great help in planning.

Footpaths were generally good, because they were in everyday use by local people as short cuts, with no other transport available, so they were well trodden and didn't need other maintenance as they do today. But when not used they quickly reverted. Bulls were a hazard and there was no legislation against them, in fact they were often used as a deterrent. Horses were also a nuisance, and much more likely to be encountered, and horse-riders used footpaths too.

But rambling then was much more catered for and popular with the general public, in particular younger people, than it is now. Organisations like the CHA (Countrywide Holidays Association), HF (Holiday Fellowship) and YHA (Youth Hostels Association) were about the only places where the sexes could get together, naturally, away from home, without raised eyebrows, and parents knew it was all respectable.

Date-specific memories

8 April 1955 (Good Friday, train to Henley). This may have been Geoffrey Stevenson's first ramble excursion, offered at five shillings (25p) return. The largest party was that led by Pago which included, apparently as usual, a large number of ladies. Some of the ramblers returned from Shiplake station having sampled the beer in the Hound of the Baskervilles pub by the station.

10 April 1955 (Easter Sunday, train to Billingshurst, Pulborough and Amberley). Possibly Geoffrey Stevenson's second excursion (or maybe his first!) when he joined Pago's group from Amberley, with lunch at the Black Rabbit pub at Offham, returning through Arundel Park to the tea room at Houghton Bridge and then the pub by Amberley station.

1 August 1955 (August Bank Holiday Monday, train to Minehead). Geoffrey Stevenson went on this Western Region excursion to Minehead. It required much stamina as they did not arrive in Minehead until quite late, having left Paddington at 10 a.m, then the return journey departed from Minehead at the quite irregular hour of 11.30 p.m, stopping in the early hours of the morning at Bristol Temple Meads for a refreshment stop, then in a siding at Swindon where the engine came off for about an hour. Even before the train reached Paddington (at about 6.30 a.m) it stopped at Goring and

Streatley to allow some really hardy people to get off and do their own ramble before catching a service train home.

20 April 1962 (train to Ardleigh, Manningtree and Bentley). Les Douglas has become well known among London ramblers with his series of Saturday Strolls, and has been joint editor of *South East Walker* and its predecessors for many years. But he started by going on some excursions that were organised by George Lockie to cater for both ramblers and railway enthusiasts in the 1950s-1960s, when the teenage Les was of the latter persuasion. On this (Les's first) excursion, as was usual on George Lockie's trips, an extension was organised for railway enthusisasts along the branch line to Hadleigh with a special train consisting entirely of brake vans: strange but true – Les still has the ticket to prove it. A more painful memory for Les from that day is that his bottle of lemonade exploded during a side-trip to the locomotive depot in Ipswich.

15 September 1963 (train to Pulborough and Amberley). In a note on a later itinerary sheet, George Platt wrote, 'A serious complaint has been received from the proprietor of an inn, that a rambler washed her muddy boots in the basin of the ladies toilet and left the basin in a deplorable state. As a result of this thoughtless and irresponsible action we have been forbidden to use this catering establishment on any future ramble and it is hoped that the person responsible will make an apology to the landlord. As we are likely to encounter muddy conditions, it cannot be stressed too strongly that it is your personal responsibility to remove all traces of mud from your footwear before entering any catering establishment. Please assist by leaving all catering establishments as you would your own home.'

22 March 1964 (coach to South Harting and Midhurst). This was the first excursion attended by Bob Goodman, who subsequently became a regular leader and a founder member of the Vanguards.

18 April 1965 (train to Axminster and Seaton). As well as being the date on which the Vanguards were established (see page 78), Bob Goodman remembers that, just after the party had set off, a milk float ran over leader Denis Hicks's foot. We don't know how serious this was, but Denis was leading again by the following October.

6 November 1966 (train to Meopham and Sole Street). This included what has gone down in the annals as 'The Pipeline Ramble'. The party that had Bob Goodman as leader and David Wright as rearguard found that part of the route (which had been clear during their survey) had been dug up for pipe laying, requiring walking a considerable distance along churned up mud, so at the end there was nearly a riot by exhausted ramblers who cursed them for leading such an awful walk.

9 April 1967 (train to Amberley and Arundel). This was Colin Saunders's first ramble excursion. He joined the Vanguards on their private ramble, which stopped for lunch at a pub in Storrington, where they all sat on the grass in the garden. He particularly remembers that there was a considerable number of attractive young women in the group, and was minded to continue with 'this rambling lark'. He also remembers Howard Johnson doing something called 'the rain dance' along the approach to Arundel Station.

30 July 1967 (train to Chilworth and Shalford). The Vanguards followed their own ramble with a lunch stop at the Plough Inn at Coldharbour. When they launched into a raucous succession of rugby songs, the regulars enthusiastically joined in and the landlord asked the Vanguards to come again soon (but they never did).

13 August 1967 (train to Petersfield and Rowlands Castle). The Vanguards hired several boats on the rowing lake at Petersfield and spent most of the time splashing each other with the oars.

21 January 1968 (train to Dorking and Holmwood). During an outbreak of foot-and-mouth disease, Bob Goodman led his party three times up Leith Hill from different directions, as it was one of the few open spaces still accessible to ramblers. It was foggy and he tried to convince the party that they were three different hills.

4 August 1968 (Battle and Crowhurst). Colin Saunders's first go at leading was not a great success – though as rearguard he was actually deputising for Howard Johnson who had briefly dived behind a bush. After crossing a stile into a wood, Colin decided (erroneously) that it was necessary to turn left immediately along a path beside a barbed wire fence. The path ran out, he climbed over the fence and looked back at the party, who were strung out and unable to move as they were caught between the barbed wire and brambles. The glares they directed at him spoke volumes, and one accused Colin of being a sadist.

15 September 1968 (train to Gomshall, Chilworth and Shalford). Due to flooding, the special train was cancelled, but some Vanguards were determined to travel. They took a service train to Redhill and changed there for Gomshall, then walked to Shere for lunch. Intending to hitch-hike to Guildford, they then set off along the road in pouring rain. Micky Kohn happened to look behind and saw an indistinct brown vehicle approaching. As it got closer, he could make out an indicator saying 'Guildford', and instinctively stuck his hand out. It was indeed a bus, and everyone was relieved to get out of the downpour.

20 April 1969 (train to Chilham, Chartham and Canterbury West). The results were announced of a competition organised by George Platt on a trip to Berwick and Polegate to celebrate his 400th excursion as organiser. The idea was to guess the total number of people who had travelled on those excursions (which turned out to be 162,992, an average of 407 per excursion), with book tokens offered to the three nearest guesses. Closest was Colin Saunders (157,563) followed by Keith Pratley (153,100) and Friedericke Kohn (Michael's mother, 171,936). Presumably, Colin's handwriting was not too clear as George published his surname as 'Sandals', which has ever since been his nickname. Special mention was made of an entry from Les Douglas guessing 100,000 ramblers, 350 dogs, 12 cats, 1 budgerigar, 3 tortoises, 212 folding prams, 72,000 rucksacks and a goldfish named Sebastian. A similar competition was organised on 28 May 1972 on the occasion of George's 20th anniversary as organiser (of 467 excursions), but sadly it only attracted six entries and no prizes were awarded.

29 June 1969 (train to Witley and Haslemere). Colin Saunders was leading a party into the Devil's Punchbowl. After he and 17 of his 75-strong party passed a crossing path near the bottom, John Grinsell led his 102-strong party along the crossing path, with the result that the majority of Colin's party were misled into joining John's, which ended up with 160 members, while Colin had no idea what had happened to the rest of his. They were reunited at Haslemere Station.

6 July 1969 (train to Billericay and Ingatestone). Colin Saunders remembers what he refers to as Bill Ramsey's 'conjuring trick' during their survey for this excursion, when Bill lifted his foot and a rabbit ran out from under it. While on the excursion itself, Frank Barker performed a disappearing trick by stepping backwards into a very deep ditch in the middle of a conversation.

10 August 1969 (train to Gomshall, Chilworth and Shalford). Party number two, with Bill Ramsey as leader, Chris Kew as rearguard and including a large contingent of Vanguards, on a very hot day made their lunch stop at the Drummond Arms pub at Albury. The Tilling Bourne flows past its garden, and the Vanguards cooled off by jumping in and furiously splashing each other. Colin Saunders's green pound notes turned red from the stain of his soaking red wallet and the shirt of a bra-less young lady became see-through. The same young lady then turned her jeans into shorts by cutting off the legs.

9 November 1969 (train to Horsley and Clandon). Following a supposed transgression of some sort by Maureen Williams, Vanguards Colin Saunders and Howard Johnson picked her up and 'pretended' to drop her in a horse trough, but they misjudged the distance and the unfortunate young lady was unintentionally dipped into the water. She was not amused!

15 February 1970 (train to Borough Green & Wrotham and West Malling). After becoming detached from their party in deep snow, Vanguards Bob Goodman, Colin Saunders and David Wright found themselves inside an abandoned army camp in Mereworth Wood, which they explored and climbed a rickety observation tower.

24 May 1970 (train to Corfe Castle and Swanage). This train ramble was notable for being George Platt's 450th as organiser, while John Grinsell celebrated his 300th as a party leader and Denis Hicks his 100th.

13 September 1970 (train to Haslemere and Liphook). On a hot day, some of the Vanguards decided to cool off by sliding down the cascade at Waggoners Wells. Bob Goodman lost his spectacles when they fell off and preceded him down the cascade. This was also the ramble on which Angela Ferrari (now Bellwood) and Sheila Webb (now Dowsett) were introduced to the Vanguards, who on the homeward journey were piling as many people as possible into their chaotic compartment, including some lying on the floor or in the luggage racks.

14 March 1971 (coach to Bildeston and Lavenham). Ian Mitchell, rearguarding for Graham Collett, was supposed to phone the expected numbers to the tea place but forgot to do so. When he realised this he valiantly forged his way from the back to the front of the party then marched quickly on in order to arrive at the tea place well ahead of the party. On arrival, however, he found the party was right behind him. To make matters worse, with some 75 members, this was one of the largest ever parties on a coach ramble, it was a very hot day, and Ian was afraid the tea place would not be able to cope – but it did!

23 May 1971 (train to Burgess Hill and Hassocks). Angela Ferrari (now Bellwood) joined party number four, led by Graham Butler. They walked in pouring rain all morning, and some people got a shock from an electric fence. Climbing Devil's Dyke's steepest slope, they hauled themselves through the mud by clinging to trees and bushes, otherwise it was a matter of sliding three steps down for every two scrambled up. One poor girl got stuck halfway and had to be rescued. Four Vanguards avoided all this by going into the pub at the foot then taking the easy path up.

27 February 1972 (train to Burgess Hill and Hassocks). David Wright remembers what became known as 'The Great George Platt footpath Fiasco', which turned out to be one of the most exciting rambles that many regulars had been on. During his survey, leader Bob Goodman encountered an angry farmer who disputed the line of the footpath and threatened to have the whole party arrested if Bob led them along it. On hearing of this, George Platt wrote to all and sundry, including the Chief Constable of Sussex, a solicitor, the press and the Ramblers' Association, and on the day of the excursion presented Bob with a sheaf of correspondence. He also presented Bob with a pile of photocopied 2½-inch maps (one for each party member) showing the line of the disputed footpath.

As the 'battlefield' drew nearer, tension mounted, but George then seemed to get cold feet and suggested using an alternative path. However, Bob (supported by Geoffrey Stevenson) insisted on using the disputed path. They passed the farm buildings, at first without being observed, but then the farmer appeared and screamed at the party. Howard Gutteridge opined that the farmer would be in his grave if he carried on like that (by which he meant that he risked suffering a heart attack) but the farmer took this as a threat and called the police, who disgracefully advised the farmer to sue for trespass and menacing behaviour. The party eventually continued along the path.

Later, after tea, they were overtaken by a police car, whose occupants demanded to know who the leader was. Fearing arrest, Bob was then only advised to take care as three walkers were recently run over by a hit-and-run motorist. Finally, to cap it all, the party missed the special train from Burgess Hill and had to catch the next service train.

15 October 1972 (Haslemere and Liphook). An item in the itinerary sheet read as follows: "A letter has been received from a Swedish girl who came out for the first time on 17th September to Rye and Winchelsea. She joined Brian Reader's party and fell for an art student and has sent a letter for onward transmission via the organiser. The only description she can give is that his name is John, he has long black hair and a flowing beard and took every opportunity to lie down and have a rest during the ramble. If anyone can answer this description and will contact the organiser he may hear something to his advantage". Sadly, we have no information as to whether anything came of this approach.

1 April 1973 (coach to St Margarets and Deal). Three parties containing over 200 ramblers arrived simultaneously on the cliffs south of Deal and poured into the town centre, leading a local resident to exclaim, "Cor blimey, war has been declared and we're being invaded!"

18 November 1973 (train to Holmwood and Ockley). Brian Reader was leading a party waiting on the platform at Holmwood Station to catch the return train at Holmwood, but it sailed straight through without stopping! There was no scheduled Sunday service so they used a bit of initiative, went up to the road, found that a Green Line coach was due, caught it, paid their fares and crammed everyone sardine-like onto the RF-type vehicle which then ran non-stop to Dorking North station leaving quite a few disgruntled prospective passengers at other stops on the way. Their faces were a picture as the bus sailed by! The Transport Committee subsequently received an apology from Southern Region.

6 October 1974 (coach to Diss). On the homeward journey, the coach was intercepted by a police patrol car, which ordered the driver to return to Diss to pick up a rambler who had been left behind. (As reported by the late Colin 'Inky' Hills.)

18 May 1975 (train to Saunderton and Princes Risborough). As all the pubs in the area were rather small, and with 72 people in his party, leader Colin Saunders had to divide them between three pubs in adjacent villages. Alan Smith adds that going was slow, resulting in a late lunch, then about 20 people hived off to go direct to the tea place, and the intended 14 mile walk had to be cut short.

8 June 1975 (train to Wadhurst and Etchingham). Alan Smith, rearguarding for Micky Kohn, had a nasty moment soon after the start when a man in his party stripped off his boots, socks and shorts (all that he was wearing) and jumped into the River Rother, stark naked. It was, apparently, a hobby of his to 'collect' rivers in this way.

29 February 1976 (coach to Harrietsham). Several Vanguards joined this excursion after spending the previous night nearby, and Les Douglas made an arrangement with the local postmaster for them to get a ride on the local postbus on the Saturday. On Sunday they made their own morning walk to join one of the official parties, and when passing through a farm near Bredgar the farmer approached and said there was no path where they intended to walk, adding that their presence could be harmful to the sheep, which would soon be lambing. He directed them to another path, which was not shown as a right of way on their maps. The walkers said they could not accept his suggestion and must follow their original plan, at which the farmer threatened to set his dog on them. John Jenkins then used words to the effect that such action would put the farmer on the wrong side of the law. They followed the intended path, and when party number two, led by Micky Kohn, went along it some twenty minutes later, the farmer came out and yelled at them, eliciting the response from Micky, "Pay no attention to him, he's illegal".

6 February 1977 (coach to Maidenhead Thicket and White Waltham). Alan Smith led party number two, replacing Les Douglas, who was ill, and Geoffrey Stevenson stood in as rearguard. On emerging from the Thicket, Geoff had disappeared, and after waiting for a while the party continued without him. The resulting delay and slow progress led to a revolt by twelve Vanguards in the party, who were anxious to get to the pub; two of them ran on ahead and the others diverted along the road. They found Geoff already at the pub – he had been looking after an old chap who had joined the wrong party. Later, Alan took a wrong turn, then Colin Saunders, discreetly relieving himself behind a bush next to the River Twy, all of a sudden slid gracefully backwards into the river up to his chest and had to wade some distance to find a place to climb out.

1 May 1978 (train to Lymington, ferry to Yarmouth, Isle of Wight). Rosie Binnie of the Polyramblers says, 'I well remember the weather on this one – absolutely terrible, with driving rain most of the day. Our party included an Indian lady in a sari and lovely sandals, and as we went up Tennyson Down the heavens opened and this poor lady got absolutely soaked – I have never seen anyone so wet in all my life! Just dripping and sodden and her beautiful black hair slithering down her shoulders, as if she had just emerged from a waterfall. Afterwards we sat in the waiting room for the ferry, shivering and soaked to the skin with sopping wet legs and underwear.

5 May 1980 (train to Aylesbury and Quainton Road). Geoffrey Waters of the Polyramblers has fond memories of this excursion, which included a ride on a special DMU (Diesel Multiple Unit), which was shuttling back and forth along the branch line to Quainton Road. After a pleasant ramble around the Vale of Aylesbury, through the villages of Quainton, Pitchcott and Oving, his party visited the steam railway centre adjacent to Quainton Road railway station for tea, where some working steam engines were on display. Then they caught the last DMU shuttle back to Aylesbury, and Geoffrey got home in time to watch the high drama of the storming of the Iranian Embassy by the SAS, live on TV!

4 May 1981 (Bamford, Hope and Edale). Geoffrey Waters writes, "This has to be my most notable rail trip of all. At least half a dozen Polyramblers attended, and what a gorgeous ridge walk we undertook from Hope – my first experience of Lose Hill, and Mam Tor. We must have covered over 10 miles, though one of us took fright at the very steep drop beside the path at Backup Edge, near Hollins Cross. After climbing and descending Mam Tor we proceeded along high ground around Castleton until we entered the narrow Cave Dale path, which is a sudden descent into Castleton. Thereupon the heavens suddenly turned grey and presented us with a very windy snowstorm through this steep, narrow dale. But, on reaching Castleton, the sun came out and we enjoyed a quick tea before setting off on buses laid on for us by the organisers to get us back to Hope station for a local train to Sheffield, then express to St Pancras. I think what makes this walk special to me is the fact that over the years I've done it at least five more times since - I could never tire of walking along that beautiful ridge again and again!"

18 October 1981 (train to Edenbridge, Penshurst Leigh and Tonbridge). The Connoisseurs Rambling Club included a ceremony to unveil an additional inscription to their late member, Freddie Fear, on the established memorial seat to Hugh E. Page at Toys Hill. The pair were life-long friends and popular train ramble leaders.

15 September 1984 (train to Carlisle and Settle). Though not included in our official programmes, this special excursion was organised by the Ramblers' Association, possibly as part of the lead-up to their Golden Jubilee. Micky Kohn remembers that it was hauled by an electric locomotive to Carlisle, then by diesel to the Ribblehead Viaduct for a photo opportunity and on to Settle. The ramblers explored the town and were treated to a talk by the comedian and keen rambler, Mike Harding, then walked the short distance to Giggleswick, where they rejoined the train for the return journey via Carnforth.

10 February 1985 (coach to Streatley and East Ilsley). When Micky Kohn and Albert Henderson surveyed this walk a few weeks beforehand, Albert visited a cheese shop in Streatley village prior to starting the walk while Micky remained outside as he found the interior somewhat malodorous. On finishing at East Ilsley, they were shocked to learn that no bus to Newbury was due for several hours (organiser Geoffrey Stevenson not having provided them with details). However, a bus with another destination suddenly turned up and its driver, on hearing of their predicament, said he was shortly going out of service but told them to wait and he would be back in a few minutes to take them to Newbury, charging the standard fare. The excursion itself took place on a fine day after a heavy snowfall, and the party passed a massive snowdrift. (As a result of their experience, Geoffrey subsequently provided leaders with detailed travel information.)

7 May 1989 (Pulborough and Amberley). There were engineering works between Horsham and Ford, so a rail replacement bus service had been arranged. Unfortunately, Southern grossly underestimated the number of passengers, as apart from the ramblers there was a large number of spectators heading for the traditional opening match of the international cricket season with a friendly at Arundel Castle between Lavinia, Duchess of Norfolk's XI and the visiting tourists

(Australia that year). The consequence was total chaos with severe delays and curtailment of the planned rambles. Micky Kohn recalls that some of the ramblers chose the soft option of visiting the Amberley Chalkpits Museum. Rather than face possible similar delays on the return journey, some chose to travel home via Hove.

14 May 1989 (train to Ham Street and Appledore). It was on this ramble that Gordon Bryant asked Brenda Allen if she would rearguard for him on 11 June 1989. This was a Saturday Stroll around Swanley, which proved to be her first experience of becoming more involved with the train rambles.

30 July 1989 (coach to Winterbourne Whitechurch and Milton Abbas). The lunchtime meal ordered by Clive Jones (who was at this time the organiser of the Other Regions train excursions) was late arriving, so he had to be left behind at the pub. This became more serious on the return journey, as there was no sign of him at Milton Abbas, with a local search proving impractical, and the coach had to return without him. It transpired that Clive had managed to get himself to Dorchester, 10 miles from Milton Abbas, but having left all his money on the coach then had to ask the booking clerk to phone his father for payment.

24 September 1989 (train to West Malling and Barming). One party had lunch at The Ship, East Malling. Just before the group set off for the afternoon walk, rearguard Brenda Allen was approached by a newcomer to the rambles and asked if she had an eye bath! However, it wasn't something that was usually carried in a first aid kit.

14 January 1990 (train to Sevenoaks and Hildenborough). Brenda Allen and Stanley Miller were the team leading party number 3, with 53 of the total 83 excursionists. They started at Hildenborough, had lunch at Shipbourne and ended at Sevenoaks. It was only Brenda's second go at leading, so the experienced Stanley led in the morning with Brenda as rearguard, then they swapped after lunch. Unfortunately, Brenda took a wrong turn and the whole party ended up on top of

One Tree Hill. A mist descended and, perhaps wrongly, she admitted that she was lost. Lots of little old ladies got really worried.

Then along came Stanley, who just walked straight past Brenda. Having been a leader and rearguard since 1978, and well known to the ramblers, a breakaway party of 36 (including all the little old ladies) followed him. The remaining 17 helped Brenda navigate to Sevenoaks station, but then it was found that Stanley, who was not carrying a map, had also taken a wrong turn and was walking away from Sevenoaks! By this time the party had fragmented and 27 were not accounted for! However, all arrived home safely and organiser Gordon Bryant told Brenda to put it down to experience if there were no complaints (and there were none).

7 May 1990 (train to High Wycombe and Saunderton). Ken Royce remembers that this was the first ramble led by Richard Kendall, with Eddie Banks as his rearguard. They had surveyed to start from Princes Risborough, but due to engineering works had to start from Saunderton instead and didn't know the way. At one point Richard realised he had taken a wrong path but found he could get to the lunch pub by a different route, so carried on. However, Geoffrey Stevenson, towards the back, told the rear of the party that the leader had gone wrong and took them along the correct route. After about a mile Richard saw the rear half crossing a field towards them and the two halves merged back together! The pub was already overwhelmed with food orders so they had to make do with beer and crisps.

27 May 1990 (train to Godalming, Milford, Witley). Party number three made a small diversion as leader Brian Reader was aware that a Surrey County Council lorry had been driven into a hedge by joy riders, demolishing a footpath sign. The ramblers tried without success to push the lorry out of the hedge.

24 June 1990 (train to Polegate and Eastbourne). After doing the survey for this excursion on 9 June, Brenda Allen and Peter Bowden arrived at Polegate station. A train slowed down at a signal box,

Peter thumbed a lift and managed to get the train to stop. At Lewes the police boarded the train and arrested three boys for theft!

14 July 1991 (train to Southease, Newhaven, Bishopstone and Seaford). Party number one had 56 out of a total of 81 ramblers! Though rather strung out at times it was very successful, but towards the end Brenda Barker and Gladys Lilli (an Argentinian lady) were deep in conversation and managed to miss which way the party went on a golf course. However, they caught the group up at the tea shop called Annie's Pantry.

15 September 1991 (train to Sawbridgeworth and Bishop's Stortford). It was suggested to one of the party, a lady who was wearing flimsy white slip-on shoes with bobbles, that she should really go on the short walk. However, she persisted in her aim to go on the longer walk and finished up being pursued by an amorous gentleman.

24 November 1991 (train to Otford and Borough Green). There were lots of engineering works that day. All three walks finished at Borough Green and all 48 ramblers attempted to board the replacement bus. Some, including the Horwills, had to wait for the next bus.

14 February 1993 (train to West Malling, East Malling and Barming). One of the problems caused by engineering works was the lack of information as to where the replacement bus would stop. After surveying for this walk on 21 January, Brenda and David Horwill waited patiently at East Malling station for the bus. It never arrived, so they crossed to the local pub for a drink where they were told, "Oh, the bus can't reach the station, you have to go down the hill to get it".

15 August 1993 (train to Maidstone East, Bearsted and Hollingbourne). Party number two, led by Brenda and David Horwill, had reached the North Kent Showground at Detling, only to discover that a clay pigeon shoot was taking place. The participants were firing over the footpath and this led to an altercation between the ramblers and the shooters, especially as rambler Denis Marshall had been hit on the shoulder by a fragment of clay pigeon. Later that evening the local police were phoned and they took appropriate action to ensure that it would not happen again.

22 August 1993 (coach to Winchcombe and Sudeley). On the survey for this excursion, due to some mix-up in the translation, Renata Howell (who is Croatian and was rearguarding for Micky Kohn) somehow bought in error a return ticket to Canterbury rather than Cheltenham, but managed to get away with it.

3 October 1993 (train to Effingham Junction and Horsley). One party suddenly encountered Sebastian Coe, now Lord Coe, the former athlete and politician, who was in charge of the 2012 Olympic Games in London. He was out walking with his daughter and two dogs, and greetings were exchanged.

12 June 1994 (train to Ham Street, Appledore and Rye). On the survey for this walk, Brenda and David Horwill had encountered an amazing path problem north of Ham Street, but nevertheless led the party along it on excursion day. The footpath sign pointed at an impenetrable hedge, but the field could be entered through a nearby gate. Then the party had to leap over a ditch and climb over a series of fences, using rudimentary stiles including carpenters' benches, where the path crossed the ends of some private gardens and a builder's yard with materials scattered across the path.

30 June 1996 (train to Wye, Chilham and Chartham). Party number one, led by Brenda and David Horwill, passed through Great Bower Farm, where, lying forlornly in a field, were a rare double-decker bus and several derelict railway carriages including the Pullman car 'Phyllis', which not long before had served as a directors' dining room for a business located next to Finsbury Park Station.

15 September 1996 (train to Eynsford, Shoreham and Otford). Pat Hills had stopped to pick blackberries on a train ramble in Kent, but when she looked round party number one, led by Brenda and David Horwill, had disappeared. However fast she walked, there was no sign of them, so she just kept walking. She eventually caught up first Geraldine Fellows, then Michael O'Reilly, who had also become separated. A fourth person joined them from another direction, but this proved to be an infamous male excursionist who was renowned for his strange behaviour. They walked on together and eventually reached a road, but had not the faintest idea where they were or where to go next. They learned later that they had gone wrong at a fingerpost. A lady who stopped nearby in a car was unable to help – or perhaps unwilling when she saw the strange man, who had become abusive, but mercifully soon went his own way. The remaining three continued along the road to a golf clubhouse, where they got a lift to Otford Station.

Meanwhile, Brenda and Jenny Hale had been searching for the missing quartet without success. They had now become separated from the party themselves, and while Jenny decided to walk to Orpington, Brenda hurried to Otford, and while running down a steep hill broke a metal boot insole. On the outskirts of Otford she bumped into David, who by now had deposited the party at the station. They went into an antiques shop which sold refreshments and found the pop singer and actor, Adam Faith, having tea there. And on arriving at the station they were reunited with the missing four!

22 June 1997 (train to Appledore and Wye). A lightning strike at the London Bridge signal box seriously delayed all trains from Charing Cross, and the rambles started an hour late. The storm caught up with the ramblers at Appledore and they were drenched. Party number one arrived late at their lunch pub at 1.50 pm, only ten minutes before closing time, but the landlord let them eat their sandwiches inside until 2.30.

31 August 1998 (train to Stansted Mountfitchet and Elsenham). A Japanese journalist was finding out what British people did for recreation and spoke to Stanley Miller. Many months later the journalist sent Stanley the book she had written, which also had a photo of him crossing a field. Unfortunately it was all in Japanese!

5 March 2000 (train to Selling and Canterbury East). During the survey on 13 February, while following the Stour Valley Walk just outside Canterbury, Brenda Horwill was bitten on the ankle by a terrier. The owner denied all responsibility – he had several dogs and claimed they were all locked up at the time, but the Canterbury police were later informed of the incident. On the way home Brenda and David called at the casualty department of Bromley Hospital but found the place in chaos, with police everywhere, as the result of a fatal stabbing involving hospital staff.

25 February 2001 (Reigate, Dorking and Deepdene). When Micky Kohn and Jenny Hale surveyed this walk on 4 February, after a pub lunch at Betchworth the afternoon walk turned out to be very muddy and heavy-going. On arrival at Brockham, Micky inspected the bus stop timetable (as one does) and discovered that a bus to Dorking was imminent; and as their enthusiasm was waning fast they could not resist the temptation to wait for and board it. Micky adds that the vehicle was an early 1950s RF type single-decker, which made the ride all the more interesting. As it turned out, the survey proved to be in vain as the planned excursion was cancelled due to an outbreak of foot-and-mouth disease (it was replaced by one to Hastings).

24 March 2002 (train to Twyford). There were problems with the trains at Paddington, remembers Roger Kemp, and the public address system mentioned something about a lorry damaging a railway bridge. Says Roger, "There was a very limited service, with very few stops. We wanted to go to Twyford and the trains were most certainly not stopping there. Abandon hope all ye who want to ramble! All eyes looked towards Geoffrey, the only person not to appear concerned – he seemed to thrive on problems. 'We'll go to Reading and see what's going on there,' he announced.

"Reading Station was very crowded, the staff had gone into hiding, and nobody knew what was going on. We needed to get back to Twyford but nothing was happening and the crowd was turning ugly. After quite some time, a London-bound train came into another platform, and Geoffrey vanished. We next saw him having a long conversation with its driver, then he called us over and we boarded the train. Said Geoffrey, 'This train is not supposed to stop at Twyford, but it is going to do so today. The driver said it was not on his timetable and refused to stop at first, but I told him that, at times like this, with all the trains up the creek, he had to use his initiative, and he eventually agreed. Mind you, he took some persuading.' "

23 March 2003 (train to Tonbridge and High Brooms). On learning that party number two would be stopping at Southborough for lunch, local rambler and councillor Maurice Knights arranged for the party to be introduced to the Mayor of Southborough, who was pleased that ramblers were supporting the local economy.

10 August 2003 (train to Ely and Littleport). The ramble took place on the hottest day of the year, and a notorious gentleman (who has been referred to earlier and caused problems whenever he came out) refused to walk any further, sat down in the middle of the path and got left behind. What happened then is not clear, but at some point he was found wandering by the local police, who found the day's itinerary in his pocket. They contacted organiser Geoffrey Stevenson, who explained the situation. It is not known how the troubled and troublesome one got home, but this was the last time anyone saw him.

Undated Memories

The Fullers Arms, now known as the Berwick Inn, stands next to Berwick Station in East Sussex. In order to arrive back in London at a reasonable hour, it was usually necessary for the homeward train to depart soon after 7 pm, and as the Sunday licensing hours in those days didn't allow pubs to open until that time, it would have been practically impossible to get a drink before boarding the train. When such a journey was due to depart from Berwick, George Platt forewarned the landlord, who would obligingly unlock the doors at about 6.45, having lined up halves and full pints of the tipples that most customers would ask for: the notoriously strong local ciders of Merrydown and Bob Luck. This could lead to some regrettable behaviour on the homeward journey: remembered incidents include the transfer of a sleeping rambler from his seat to the luggage rack, the removal of a light bulb resulting in all the carriage lights going out, doing the conga along the corridor (when one of its participants had his shorts down around his ankles) and even, most disgracefully, the misappropriation of a guard's green flag.

Even George Platt was affected occasionally. On one occasion he left the pub and leant on the gates of the level crossing. "Do not lean on the gates!" he shouted as they started to close. Moving onto the platform, he yelled "Stand back from the edge of the platform!" then promptly threw up over the track.

The tree on the line. Some time around 1970, a Southern Region homeward journey from Balcombe was brought to a halt by a tree having fallen across the line. George Platt came along the train asking for volunteers to help remove it, then warned us to "Mind the electrified rail" as we clambered down to the trackside. Imagine that happening in today's Health & Safety conscious times!

The Great White Hunter and Daphne regularly attended excursions during the 1960s. They invariably wore baggy khaki shorts and sola topis (pith helmets worn by game hunters). They didn't join a party, preferring to go off on their own. He would stride on ahead, rucksack-free, while poor Daphne struggled along behind, weighed down by a huge rucksack with a dangling teapot. On one occasion (Winchester and Shawford, 29 June 1968) they just missed the homeward train and he was heard to yell, 'Dammit, Daphne, you've made us miss the train again!'

"The train at Platform 2 is not for normal passengers – do not board this train!" was the rather startling announcement at East Croydon once, after giving details of its departure time and destination.

"You'd better let me on – I'm the driver!" Said when one of George Platt's officious henchmen was loudly and forcefully preventing members of the public from boarding the special train at Waterloo.

The Undertaker. A gentleman who always wore very sombre clothes, including a long, dark overcoat, was generally known as 'The Undertaker'. He was often accompanied by his similarly attired mother. During the homeward journey on a coach ramble, he felt unwell and wanted to get out, but the driver refused to stop on a motorway. The door was opened, The Undertaker sat on the step and leaned out, held in place by Geoffrey Stevenson hooking his stick around the unfortunate man's collar.

Love-in-a-mist! A couple of ramblers, of mixed gender, found themselves detached from their party in thick fog. On a hill, they sat down to rest, became entwined and got rather carried away. After a while they heard people laughing and looked up to find that the fog had cleared and another party was passing along the footpath below, enjoying the view!

Personal memories

Angela Bellwood started rambling in 1970, when she was Angela Ferrari. When attending evening classes for Italian at Morley College, she met Sheila Webb (now Dowsett), who persuaded her to go with the Morley College Rambling Club on a cold and muddy Sunday, wearing lace-up shoes and carrying a shopping bag! They continued going with Morley College until they discovered the train rambles, and on the excursion to Haslemere and Liphook on 13 September 1970 joined party number one, led by John Grinsell. The heavens opened at lunchtime and they decided to walk back to Haslemere along the road, meeting up with two Vanguards, Leslie Smart and Pauline James – see this date above for further details.

Joan Brown had enjoyed roaming the hills during her wartime evacuation to North Wales. On her return to London she missed her rambling so started going on the ramblers' excursions, and continued with them for many years, latterly with the 'Cons' (the Connoisseur Rambling Club), for whom she was rambles organiser.

David Dowsett remembers a ridiculous situation that arose on a ramble that ended at a place called Cobblers Hill near Wendover. The owner of a bungalow came out as the party walked along a lane, a right of way. He pointed to a strip of grass across the lane and said, "You can't cross this, it's private". "How can it be, when the rest of the lane is a right of way?" said David. However, the man insisted that there was no right of way, so to keep him quiet David and Bill Ramsey carried the party members across the strip of grass, while the man and his wife looked on. "Where are you going?" enquired the wife. "Cobblers!" said Bob Goodman. "There's no need to be rude," she replied.

Frank Dring led two walks for Morley College Rambling Club on excursions to the Peak District on 5 October 1975 and 2 October 1977. They were very long days, leaving St Pancras at about 8.45 a.m and returning at about 10.30 p.m. On the second trip he particularly enjoyed a roast meal at a farmhouse for only thirty 'bob' (shillings, or £1.50 – equivalent to about £6.50 in 2014).

Paul Frances was a regular attender on the excursions, then when he moved to Hungerford he offered to lead when they occasionally went in that direction. On one occasion he had informed the Pelican Inn at Froxfield that about 25 people would require lunch, but 41 turned up on a lovely day and he had no opportunity to warn them. Despite the extra business they weren't pleased, but sent someone to Marlborough to buy more baguettes. Paul's brother-in-law, Peter Camfield, used to organise afternoon teas for the ramblers at local halls, such as the Croft Hall in Hungerford and the village halls at Inkpen and Chilton Foliat.

David Griffin vividly remembers Mike Herniman sinking up to his calves in thick mud and being totally unable to move. After much effort, his fellow ramblers managed to extricate Mike, but minus boots. Further digging eventually freed the boots, but they were so mud-caked and filthy that Mike had to walk uncomfortably in his socks for some time until he reached a stream for a good clean-up operation.

Bridget Harper was a popular leader on the excursions, renowned for a fast pace, despite her diminutive size. On one ramble, it had been raining very heavily and a plank bridge across a stream had been swept away. The stream had become fast-flowing, and was more than boot-deep. Bridget assured her party that a bridge really had been there on the survey. Said Bridget, "It's up to you what we do now. You've got a choice: the next bridge is one-and-a-half miles away, so an extra three miles; or we cross the water here. Quite up to you, I don't mind either way." So into the water they all jumped – it beat an extra three miles walk!

Another time Bridget's party came across an inscription on a wall, written in some unfamiliar script. "It's a song. In Welsh," she said, and proceeded so sing it – in Welsh!

On another occasion, Bridget, as rearguard, was some way behind those of us at the front. She dropped her Thermos flask, which shattered into a thousand pieces. The expletives that resulted, in Bridget's cultured tones, carried all the way to the front of the party.....and have had to be deleted!

Dick Hutchins, who died aged 97 in January 2013, was one of the early ramblers' excursionists, and his daughter Madeline Hutchins has kindly allowed us to quote from the life history notes that he wrote: "I joined the Ramblers' Association in 1935, aged 19/20, while a student of law at the London School of Economics. Nearly every weekend I went out walking in the countryside. Southern Railways ran special ramblers' trains and you would go out to one station and come back from another, which was quite a feature in those days. I remember Tom Stephenson talking on one walk."

As a 17-year-old student, Dick heard with great excitement about the Kinder Scout trespass in 1932 and became a highly respected activist for both the Ramblers and the Open Spaces Society. His achievements included: walking 156 miles from London to Fishguard in 1936 to catch the ferry home to County Cork for the summer vacation; serving in the Second World War, retiring in 1946 as a Lieutenant Colonel; writing a book about the National Parks and Access to the Countryside Act of 1949; organising Derbyshire County Council's survey of footpaths under that act; negotiating the purchase of the old railway line that became the Tissington Trail in 1971; and establishing the Blue Peris Mountain Centre in Snowdonia in 1977 on behalf of Bedford Borough Council.

Roger Kemp's first excursion on 1 April 1956 went to Wareham and Corfe Castle, when he was just 8 years old, with his mother. He remembers the steam trains, and that they were good days out. Young as he was, he used to get a glass of Woodpecker cider at the pub – in those days he was not allowed inside but there was always a kind person willing to oblige.

Roger and his mother travelled on several excursions at that time. Once they travelled down in the guard's van, together with some young men who were laughing and joking – an early incarnation of the Vanguards perhaps? He stopped going regularly on the excursions for some time after that, but went occasionally. Then between about 1982 and 1988 Roger went on quite a number with his own children, and again from 1993. But in 1998 his mother had a very serious stroke and he was unable to go again until after she died in 2003. He has been a regular since, including on Geoff's Jaunts.

Roger recalls one lovely summer day when a woman turned up for a conducted train ramble dressed for a day out in town, complete with the fashion item of the day: stiletto heels. Says Roger, "I had never seen her before and don't recall ever seeing her again. My guess is that she was new to rambling.....only a guess, mind. I heard Bridget Harper's instruction on the Rambles Hotline ringing in my ears: 'Wear *walking* shoes or boots'. But the amazing thing was, the lady completed the walk, for on a day like that you could get away with doing it in bare feet.....you could, but you wouldn't want to do it again!"

Roger also remembers a ramble on the Isle of Wight, led by Geoffrey Stevenson, who was accompanied by one of his blind friends with a new guide-dog. "We passed a small mobile home site, then entered the disused railway cutting that leads out of Shanklin. The blind man said it would be nice to let the dog off its harness for a while to give her a bit of exercise, as she was new to guiding and not used to things yet. After about five minutes, it was decided that the dog had better be put back in the harness. One problem though.....where was the dog? Nobody knew. The walk would have to stop right here until the dog was found. We then remembered another dog passing in the opposite direction with its owner in tow, so some of us walked back and got as far as the mobile homes, where we saw the dog owner who had passed us earlier. 'Have you seen a dog?' we asked, only to realise that the dog was sitting there. The man said, 'I found the guide-dog disc, and have just called the police. I realised it was serious. I suppose that guide-dog must have followed my dog.' "

Micky Kohn started going on the ramble excursions in his early teens with his mother, Friedericke, in the late 1950s and later became a regular member of the Vanguards, an excursion organiser and a member of the Transport Committee. He had been taught to use OS maps at school, and when he started rambling bought the relevant sheets and usually walked just in front of the leader (often John Grinsell), trying to guess which paths would be taken, thereby improving his map-reading skills. Micky started leading on the trains in 1967, then on the coaches in 1975 – often as a result of Geoffrey Stevenson phoning late in the evening when Micky was too drowsy to decline!

Micky particularly enjoyed travelling on the coaches, in a seat behind the driver, usually beside Harold Lawrence. On one occasion it was necessary to borrow a vehicle from Empress Coaches of Cambridge Heath; on the way out of London, heading west, it broke down and the driver, fearing a fire, got everyone out of the coach; Geoffrey Stevenson took it upon himself to direct traffic around the stricken vehicle, but in the end they were able to continue.

On another occasion, a Grey-Green Leyland Leopard coach had to stop as its engine was overheating. On looking back, Micky spotted an empty coach and (more in humour than in hope) thumbed a lift from it. Much to his surprise, the driver stopped and Len King arranged for it to transport the ramblers to their destination.

One of the regular drivers was Alf Page, who drove his personally allocated coach for Orange Luxury Coaches out of Brixton Garage, commuting by car from his home in Watford. He was an excellent driver who enjoyed his days out with the ramblers and became friendly with many of them. Alf's intimate knowledge of London streets enabled him to take back routes to avoid traffic problems. He also drove for the Victor Sylvester Ballroom Orchestra.

Micky also remembers a train excursion from Liverpool Street to somewhere in Essex (possibly Southminster). This being one of those diesel multiple units in which passengers could look ahead through the driver's cab, Micky was sitting in a front seat and had a grandstand view of what transpired. At Shenfield, the train diverted onto a north-side loop track on which a train could either be routed back onto the main line or through an underpass to the Southend Victoria and Southminster branch. The signalman misdirected the train back onto the main line, and the driver had to stop and get out to correct the signalman.

Diana Lucas (better known to excursionists as Diana Hack, daughter of organiser Arthur) has a few memories of the excursions from her childhood, especially the party bats encouraging you to join a walk of varying difficulty and distance. She recalls:

"My dad always went for the longer walks, 15 miles plus, so I had to follow suit. I remember they were always sociable but stepped out with a purpose. My mum recalled an occasion when dad had to run and vault over a hedge when being chased by a bull in a field.

"One of my favourite walks was from Berwick station across the South Downs. At the Cricketers pub in Berwick I remember you walked through the door of the public bar and immediately there was a dartboard on the wall. I recall narrowly missing someone walking in when aiming for a double top. There's a church near the pub and at the back of the church there's a view across fields towards the coast. I understand the Ramblers were thinking of placing a seat there in memory of dad, but my mum thought it would be more fitting to continue to work to dad's ideals and give enjoyment to all ramblers and make it possible for them to appreciate the attractions of the beautiful English countryside which was a great part of his life.

"I remember a few people from those days – Geoff Stevenson, Howard 'Gus' Gutteridge, Micky Kohn, George and Bridie Platt and

The Cricketers Arms at Berwick, East Sussex.

an older gentleman who took his dog on the walks. When I have since owned dogs local rambler groups here in the Midlands don't allow them which is a shame."

Alex Masson started going on the train excursions in 1979 when rambling seemed so free-and-easy and there were few rules and worries about health and safety. He remembers a gentleman who went on the coaches dressed like a 'pukka sahib' (British colonial administrator) and who had been, he said, a soldier, mountaineer and big-game hunter. For Alex, the words of Bridget Harper on the Rambles Hotline provided a suitable epitaph for the excursions: "Everyone is welcome and there's no charge!"

Ros Pool went on the excursions during the early 1960s, usually with other members of the West London RA Group, and remembers in particular two incidents involving the unforgettable George Platt. On one to Glynde and Berwick, people rushed (as usual) from downing their strong ciders at the Fullers Arms to catch the waiting train at the adjacent Berwick station. Just as the train started to pull out, someone told George that his wife, Bridie, wasn't on board and he yelled to stop the train.

The other took place after an ascent of Blackdown Hill: the ramblers had arrived at Haslemere station with nearly an hour to wait for the homeward excursion train. They decided to catch an earlier one, but George insisted that their special tickets would not be valid and they must pay the single fare, much to the annoyance and consternation of the station clerk, who did not have enough printed tickets and had to write most of them by hand. And it transpired that some of the party had got past George and travelled on the earlier train without paying extra.

Bill Ramsey's first excursion was by coach to Long Melford and Clare on 26 July 1964. He was then an innocent 16-year-old, but soon fell in with the Vanguards and was converted to their way of thinking, especially after visits to the Fullers Arms at Berwick Station. "On one homeward journey I joined a conga along the train when somehow my shorts ended up around my ankles. Being lithe and athletic at that time, I grasped the handles of the seats and swung myself up and placed my boots on the ceiling, while Dave Crake played a guitar to accompany the Vanguards' usual singing of rugby songs. This resulted in George Platt issuing a warning on the next journey's itinerary: 'There will be no gymnastics and playing of musical instruments on future excursions' ".

On an excursion to Lewes and Seaford, the Vanguards thought it great fun to wade across Cuckmere Haven at low tide. As Bill did this, he found that the current was stronger than expected, forcing him into deeper water, so that his trousers were getting soaked, but he somehow managed to remove his trousers in midstream and remain upright, while non-ramblers out for a stroll took photos. Bill later stood on a tall breakwater post to pose for more photos.

On one homeward journey, the train had a buffet car. The counter was wet, so the Vanguards dried it with Bill – that is to say, they picked him up, lay him on the counter and wiped him up and down it.

Bill Ramsey, a regular leader between 1966 and 1975, demonstrates his poise and agility by ascending a breakwater at Cuckmere Haven, supported by Pat Baker.

Incidentally, that buffet car unusually had Wild West saloon type swing doors.

On a Merry-Maker trip to Tenby, the train was met by the Mayor. Bill was introduced to him by Robin Ray as 'Sir William Ramsey'. Said His Worship, 'We're very honoured to have you visit us, Sir William', and allowed himself to be photographed with the fraudulent knight together with Pauline James, another Vanguard, who hailed from Swansea and was dressed in her national costume. Even to this day Bill is known to the Vanguards as Sir William.

One day a party was struggling to reach the station in time for the homeward journey, Bill raced ahead with David Wright and Bob Goodman, to get George to hold the train. When George refused and started shutting the doors, they went along the train re-opening them. The party caught the train.

Bill remembers a rather strange leader who, in order to avoid forking out for a collection on behalf of the Ramblers' Association, said he would pretend to be a suitcase and climbed into the luggage rack.

Brian Reader was leading a walk from Great Missenden and set off after the usual few minutes milling about in the station yard sorting out the various parties. After a mile or so they caught up a blind man and his guide dog who had been on the same train. He obviously had a good memory of his regular route, for he could tell Brian what the next stile was made of, whether he would have to lift his dog over it, where to turn etc. Says Brian, "We discovered that we were going the same way for the next mile before their routes diverged, so I invited the blind man, in view of his knowledge, to lead the party until that point, and explained to the party what was happening. And then we had an extremely thrilled blind man in charge, so much so that instead of following his usual route he joined us for the rest of the day to learn some new paths."

On a Merry-Maker excursion to the Peak District, Brian Reader was leading a party of 80 from Bamford to Win Hill with wife Gill as rearguard. Itineraries given out on these excursions always carried a rider to the effect that routes could be changed at a leader's sole discretion. Brian intended to go up the eastern arm of Kinder Scout, circling round the edge to the northern side then across the top to Ringing Roger before descending to Edale. The weather was dry but the cloud was low, hovering just above the Kinder plateau. Says Brian, "I told the party that if there was any sign of the cloud coming down I would change the walk to a lower route. As we approached decision point, the cloud had stayed at the same level and the party all wanted to go up, so I said that was what we would do but that we MUST stick together and not lose sight of the person in front. I've never had an easier party to lead! We got to Ringing Roger an hour ahead of schedule. We then gave the party a choice: they could either descend with Gill by the intended route, or do an impromptu walk extension with me, descending nearer the top of Grinds Brook and following the Pennine Way into Edale. Four of the party went with Gill while I took the remaining 76 – these included Geoff

Stevenson, who acted as temporary rearguard until the top of the descent where we switched roles so that I could be last off the hill."

Carl Roe has fond memories of one of Bob Mulholland's bank holiday excursions to the Wye Valley, when they returned overnight, alighted at Goring & Streatley and walked up Streatley Hill to sunbathe before returning to Paddington later in the morning. He also remembers leading a party of over 60 from Selling in the early 1960s and walking to Chartham for lunch then on to Canterbury for tea. It was in May and all the blossom was out in the orchards.

Ken Royce (who sadly died in June 2013 aged 83) had fond memories of leaders Freddie Fear, who would come from behind to be first up a hill, and 'Mr R.E. Smith', who consistently refused to allow his first name to be published, but was known to close friends as Roe. The latter was known for his fondness of darts, and any pub that had a dartboard would find him spending most of the lunch stop 'on the oche'. Ken and Roe were among the gathering at fellow rambler Alec Cole's wedding, which took place in Streatham, but the wedding breakfast was at a restaurant in Soho. Afterwards some of the men continued to a nearby pub with a dartboard, and Roe (who had been imbibing rather freely) was shooting his arrows like loose cannons in all directions around the bar.

Another memory of 'Mr Smith', from *Mike Herniman*, is of him confidently shouting "It's this way, follow me!" then diving into thick holly bushes and leaving the party standing in amazement.

Ken Royce also remembers leading a party of 30 in 1961 that visited a pub in Kent called the Leather Bottle. Ken Thornton was leading another party of 60 that was due to visit another pub in the area called the Spotted Dog, but on arrival found the landlord, a Mr Leppard, barring entry. He said, "You can't bring that lot in 'ere". So Ken T took them on to the Leather Bottle, now crammed to the rafters with 90 ramblers.

John Stebbings' first excursion was on a train to Amberley, when he joined an excursion led by John Grinsell. John says, "He was a very affable man and a great ambassador for the Ramblers' Association. I enjoyed such a good walk among good company that I came again. John was almost always there, although such was the variety of leaders that I didn't always go with him."

Of George Platt, John remembers the time in Sussex when his party approached the station with the return train about to leave. In order to get there in time, they scrambled over a fence and crossed some waste ground. George roared, "You must go round the proper way", but if they had done so they would have missed the train!

On another train ramble, John Stebbings and two others broke away from their party, but on nearing the station found their way blocked by barbed wire. John and one other managed to get around the wire, but the third decided to climb over and soon realised that its purpose was to fence off a sea of mud, into which she deeply sank. It took half an hour to extricate her, and then her shoes, and they missed the train.

John remembers, of a coach ramble in the Chilterns, that the leader set off after lunch at a cracking pace in order to get to the tea stop in time. On reaching a wood, they accidentally split into three groups, some with the leader, some with the rearguard, and some including John in a middle group, who went astray. But eventually, after much shouting and whistle-blowing, they were reunited and reached the tea stop in good time.

On a coach ramble in Hertfordshire, John and some friends hived off from the party and told Geoffrey Stevenson that they were going to visit Buntingford. "Ah," said Geoff, "in that case can this young lady from Australia join you? She would like to find her grandmother's grave in Buntingford church." And she did!

Geoffrey Waters was only 22 when he joined the Polytechnic Rambling Club (popularly known as the Polyramblers) in June 1978. When the Club committee met, it would usually include one of these trips on the forthcoming Polyramblers programme, as they found that their organisation was superb. He recalls going on several trips in the late 1970s and the 1980s, and the main thrill for him in his early 20s was the excitement of travelling to places for the first time.

One notable excursion he attended in July 1989 went by coach to Charlbury in Oxfordshire and included the opening of a new footpath through the previously forbidden territory of Wychwood Forest.

Pat Williamson was born in Bath but moved to Scotland when she was young. In her youth she did a fair amount of mountain and hill climbing, but through visits to London over the years came to know London quite well. When she moved to live there she found the south fairly flat and uninteresting but thanks to the ramblers quickly came to appreciate the very wide variety of countryside there and the enormous amount of work put in by the ramble organisers. The various ramble leaders (one or two rather eccentric) also did so much to make the walks interesting. The North and South Downs were particular favourites. She loved the pub lunches and found it hard to believe that they were able to eat outside in December! She hated to miss any of the rambles in the seventeen years she lived in London, not only because she enjoyed the exercise but also because she made some good friends, with whom she still keeps in touch.

David Wright was introduced to the train excursions by his old school friend, Bob Goodman – he thinks it may have been the excursion to Eridge, Crowborough and Jarvis Brook on 22 November 1964, or possibly the one to Sevenoaks on 24 January 1965. Whichever (and typically of two future Vanguards), they decided to take a short cut to the pub, going across country and having to negotiate a fenced railway line, a river and a forest.

On a coach excursion to Cambridge, David remembers an altercation between Geoffrey Stevenson and a farmer who insisted that there was no right of way across his land. Geoff showed him the map as proof but the farmer was having none of it. David said, with impeccable logic, "Look, Geoffrey Stevenson is always right, and if he's right, you must be wrong". The farmer was non-plussed, and the party continued on its way.

More memories of 'Geoff o'Stick'

Much of the following is reproduced or adapted from the encomium for Geoffrey Stevenson that appeared in the Autumn 2010 issue of *South East Walker*.

Golfo Chrysanthopoulou, a regular on Geoff's Jaunts:

Geoffrey's knowledge and love for the countryside was amazing. He worked hard to plan, organise and vary his country routes for us. He stopped at points of interest and gave us a brief history of a building, a disused railway, a monument and so on. All the information made his walks special, and this is proven by his longstanding loyal supporters. They owe a big thank you to Geoffrey, and his walks kept me away from hospitals and surgeries.

Chris Hall, a former Ramblers' Association president and secretary:

Geoff is present in my memories of the RA just after I took over as secretary early in 1969, when our offices were in Finchley Road. Geoff came there for meetings of the former Southern Area's executive committee. You could not call him an assertive or noisy member; this and his slight build led the unperceptive to overlook him, but he was always ready to argue his corner, and his allegiance to the ideal of a militant RA dedicated to defending and expanding the rights-of-way network was never in doubt.

Kate Ashbrook, General Secretary of the Open Spaces Society and a former RA chairman:

Geoff was very much a part of my roles with both the RA and the OSS. For the Society, he attended nearly every AGM within living memory and could be relied upon to vote for motions calling for tough action in defence of paths and open spaces. And he would contact me regularly, in my capacity as footpath secretary for Bucks, Milton Keynes and West Middlesex, with handwritten reports and maps of path problems that he had encountered in our patch. He knew the network intimately, having researched and claimed many of the paths. And a few weeks later he would be sure to check that I had acted on his reports. He was persistent and extremely knowledgeable, and he got things done – all with a delightful twinkle.

Graham Collett, a long-standing friend and fellow Vanguard:

Geoff was best known for his role as coach rambles organiser for the RA's Southern (later Inner London) Area, which he carried on conscientiously for many years right up until they had to stop. I rearguarded for him on a number of walks and he always sent me a postcard beforehand giving the train and bus times for the survey. They were meticulously worked out, using the timetables of the Westminster Reference Library, and he used to regularly chastise the librarians for having out-of-date bus timetables.

We had some great times together on the surveys and occasionally had one too many drinks at the lunch pub. I remember one survey in the Golden Valley (near Stroud, Glos) which included a section of the disused canal near Sapperton Tunnel on a very hot summer's day. Geoff had over-imbibed on the draft cider and I had a severe hay fever attack, and we both ended up incapably rolling around in the undergrowth!

Colin Saunders, another long-standing friend and fellow Vanguard:

I sometimes had to phone Geoff at work, and he would hesitantly answer 'Yachting World', as if he was surprised to be working for such a publication, where he looked after classified advertising – anyone less like a yachtsman would be difficult to imagine. On the survey for a coach ramble to Great Dunmow, Essex, in 1972, for which I was Geoff's rearguard, he kept falling into a very deep ditch soon after imbibing a substantial amount of cider at the lunch pub, and I had great difficulty pulling him out.

John Stebbings often joined Geoff's party on excursions and recalls that his regular rearguard, John Jenkins, would sometimes calm him down whenever he got a bit excited over something, like an obstreperous farmer. Much later, John Stebbings renewed his acquaintance with Geoff when he joined the committee of the RA's

Inner London Area in about 1992. Previously Geoff had seemed older than he looked, but now seemed younger than he looked! John says, "I last saw him in University College Hospital, suffering from cancer. With typical bluntness, he told me 'It's no good beating about the bush – it's terminal.' A leader to the end, he would take parties of his many visitors around his top floor ward showing them the magnificent views over London."

Roger Kemp got to know Geoffrey well during the later years of the excursions, and during Geoff's Jaunts. "On one occasion Geoff vanished. He had been at the back, then simply disappeared - there one moment, gone the next. When we noticed we waited.....and waited.....and waited. Then we started to walk back, maybe he'd been kidnapped: you read about that sort of thing in the papers, happens a lot on rambles! A few moments later he came striding towards us, swinging his stick with a little more enthusiasm than usual. 'What happened to you?' we called, and Geoff uttered these immortal words: 'I got lost.' It was the only time we ever heard him say that.

"Geoff used to talk about the Sixties television version of *The Forsyte Saga*, in which Soames was played by Eric Porter. Soames is not a very pleasant character, and Eric Porter was generally thought to have acted the part well. Geoff recalled being with a rambling group near Stratford-on-Avon, walking along the riverbank. They were nattering away when a window was abruptly thrust open to reveal Mr Angry complaining about the noise, and saying he was trying to sleep, as 'some of us have to work later'. And that, as Geoff later recalled, was the only time he personally encountered Mr Eric Porter.

"A BBC Radio 4 lady reporter came on one ramble and interviewed Geoffrey. With no hint of embarrassment, straight-faced, he told her, 'I couldn't possibly stay at home on a Sunday listening to the radio, I'd be bored stiff!'

"Whenever possible, Geoffrey liked to venture into a church – the buildings fascinated him. On one occasion, many years ago, he was challenged by a somewhat overbearing woman who said she owned the land, and this was a private church.....her church.....She Who Must Be Obeyed! 'But it's the parish church,' argued Geoffrey. 'You cannot have a *private* parish church – it's for the community.' The church was near Wimpole Hall, the home of Elsie Kipling Bambridge. That was the time Geoffrey took on the daughter of Rudyard Kipling. In later years the rambles passed her grave.....nobody challenged us then!"

Just before Geoffrey died in 2010, Roger told him that the first excursion he could remember going on was by steam train to Corfe Castle as a young boy. Straightaway Geoffrey said, "That would be in 1956" – his memory was still as sharp as a tack – and on subsequently checking our Appendix A (see page 2), Roger has established that this was indeed the excursion to Wareham and Corfe Castle on 1 April 1956.

This photo of Geoffrey Stevenson appeared in the 'You' supplement of The Mail on Sunday on 24 February 1985. It accompanied a feature on the ramblers' excursions by their reporter Sally Brompton and photographer Homer Sykes, when they joined Geoff's party on the excursion to Merstham and Redhill on 6 January.

[Reproduced by kind permission of The Mail on Sunday and Homer Sykes.]

Some memories of Geoff's Jaunts

Many thanks to Roger Kemp for all these.

1) Keith Evans and I were up in the Chilterns on a survey, miles from anywhere – even hermits would have felt lonely – and it was a hot day. Then we came across an isolated cottage, with a lady tending to her garden. Said Keith, in a tone somewhat louder than a stage whisper, "I wonder if there are any cafés around here". As if! The lady stopped weeding and looked at us timid rural travellers. "Are you thirsty?" she asked. "Would you like some tea?" I didn't know Keith could look so embarrassed. "Well, er….." he stuttered, but she was gone. Within moments, a man was sent out to set up a table, covered with a pretty table cloth, right next to the footpath. The man then brought out a pair of garden chairs. To be honest, he didn't seem over-impressed by us, you'd think he thought we had a bloody nerve. The lady returned with bone china tea-cups and saucers, and told the man to fetch some cakes. He grunted, and sort of smiled, but we didn't like the look of those bared teeth! We ate the cake, drank the tea, discussed the ethics of leaving a tip, then called out our thanks…..and legged it!

2) We were being led by someone from a local group and lunch was at a pub that had just won a prize for good food. It was packed and there were long delays for meals. John McGahern and I went down the road to another pub, ordered food and beer and paid in advance. Once we had finished our meal, we thought we'd better rush back to the first pub, in case the others were waiting for us. However, as we left the pub, we were loudly challenged by the landlord: "You haven't paid!" he shouted in front of everyone. You could hear a pin drop. "Yes, we have," said John. "Did you think we were about to do a runner?" The bar erupted into laughter, but the landlord was not amused. Back to the prize-winning pub, but things were not going too well there either. The rest of the group were still waiting for their food, and it was now time to set off for the afternoon walk.

3) We had to enter a field and it was extremely muddy, especially around the five-bar gate. Some of us tried to find another way

around. The rest waited to follow Geoffrey Stevenson. Keith Evans was growing shorter by the second, then we realised he was fast sinking into the deep mud. Valiant effects had to be made to retrieve his boots from the morass.

4) Lunch over, it was time to leave the pub. Being good ramblers, we had removed our muddy boots, and some of us had left them by the entrance. While we were re-booting ourselves, Andrew Ward said his boots had vanished, and he could not see the funny side of it. He stood there in his socks and said, "That's that, I'll have to get a taxi home. People who steal boots ought to be horse-whipped along the whole of the Pilgrims' Way." And he made it absolutely clear he had no intention of walking in his socks for the remainder of the day. Then we found one unclaimed pair of boots, but they were far too small for Andrew. Geoffrey Stevenson told everyone to check their boots, in case they were wearing the wrong ones. Andrew said his boots were very big, surely no one could have them on without knowing, so it must be a boot thief – horse-whipping was too good for them, tarring-and-feathering maybe. Then one of the men said his boots felt a bit on the large side....

5) Bernard Smith never as much as glances at a map, but he has a good sense of direction. Once, we were halfway through an afternoon walk when Barbara Marsh suddenly realised that she had left some vital item at the lunch pub. "I'll take you back," said Bernard, and he was able to retrace the exact route we had just followed.

6) It was Golfo Chrysanthopoulou's first walk with us. We were on Box Hill, which is of course popular walking country. Not long before lunch we passed another group and exchanged a few words before continuing on our way. Then it began to snow. When we reached our lunch pub, the King William IV at Mickleham, we realised that one of our number was missing. It was the new lady.....we'd lost the new lady! Only had her five minutes and we'd lost her! Perhaps she got bored, perhaps we had upset her, perhaps she's building a snowman..... Some time later Golfo came into the pub and

explained that, when we stopped earlier to speak to the other group, she had accidentally joined them and only found out when they ended their walk in a car-park. Golfo had a copy of our itinerary, and the other group directed her to our pub.

7) Always keep to the right of way, we are told. But sometimes this can be a mite tricky. A few years ago we came to a field that was flooded to a depth of at least six inches in water that looked less than inviting. Someone decided that the way to deal with that was to cross the field by walking carefully, crabwise, along the wire fence, with its stout wooden posts, and we managed it without anyone falling in. But at the far end we were met by a thick, impenetrable mire – a real Slough of Despond. If we had possessed mobiles then, the Samaritans would have received quite a few calls!

What we did have was an audience in the form of a local lady. "You can't get through there", she called. Thanks for that, we thought, we might be townies but we had worked that out. She waved casually towards some adjacent farmland: "But you can get through there." One of our number pointed out that where she indicated was private land. "But we can't, we must keep to the right of way," said someone. (Though it was not mentioned that we had omitted to do so when clambering along that fence earlier!) "Oh yes you can!" persisted the lady. "You can, because you have the owner's permission – I own all this land." We touched our forelocks and continued over her land, and have spoken highly of her ever since. I hope we didn't damage her fence.

8) On one occasion we came across a footpath through an alleyway that was thoroughly overgrown with thorny, rose-like bushes. We often successfully fought our way through such obstructions, and that was what Geoffrey Stevenson decided we should do here. He was very fond of keeping public rights of way open, was Geoffrey. So I set to with my trusty secateurs – and wished I hadn't. Twenty minutes later I was still cutting, now soaked in blood, sweat and tears, with the rest of the party close behind. Then someone said we were now about one-third of the way through, whereupon I (cut,

bruised, cheesed off and thinking about taking up stamp collecting, or anything that didn't involve thorns) cried "Enough's enough – we're beaten." So we went back, walked along the road for 30 yards and found a riding stables. We asked a lady if we could come through there. "Of course you can," she said. "Everyone does, there is no other way!" Geoffrey later got some council men with chainsaws to sort out our path. Strange thing is, we have never been back, but for weeks afterwards I was still pulling out thorns from my fingers, a martyr to the cause.

9) What is the best way to get mud off your boots? John McGahern was passing a man using a power-hose to wash his car. John's very muddy boots were clean in a jiffy.

10) Listen to the locals! On a survey, Keith Evans and I visited the excellent Swan in Little Chart and were perusing the menu when an elderly local man called Archie, a born-and-bred Kentishman (or maybe a Man of Kent?) said, "Ask for the rabbit pie – I swear by it". There was no such thing on the menu, but. Keith asked anyway and was presented with rabbit pie. We have been back to the pub more than once, but no Archie and no rabbit pie. Been upsetting some people with his swearing, maybe.

11) Our party had left the countryside and was now walking along a quiet residential street, where nothing much happens and not a soul was around, save us. Then things changed. Pat Hills tripped and injured her leg so badly that a hospital was needed. No call boxes around, no mobiles then, and not a human being in sight. And the best person to deal with the situation was Pat herself, as she's a former nurse. However, before panic could set in, the door of the corner house was thrust open by a lady, who called over to us that she had seen what happened and her husband was a GP! The moral of this story is, "Never knock a curtain-twitcher!"

12) Surveys can be memorable. For example, on one that Keith Evans and I did around Sevenoaks, everything was going well – too well. We were about two miles from Sevenoaks station with just a bit of

woodland to get through, looking forward to finishing and having a nap on the train. We took a wrong turn but soon got back on to the right route to leave the wood, only to find our path completely blocked. The right of way was on the map, but the closure looked very official. So we worked out the right direction and struck out to look for an exit. And we walked on and on and on. It was getting dark and neither of us had a torch. Keith's laminated map was becoming invisible, as was the very path. Wherever we walked, Sevenoaks still looked about two miles away.

I said, "If we get to a road, will it be lit?"

"Probably not," moaned Keith.

"Oh great, two miles of pitch black road. Do you think we should scribble our wills?" "I can't see to write!" retorted Keith.

And on we went through the longest wood in the British Isles - must be 25 miles long, or that's what it felt like. And no dog walkers, no.....

"Look, what's that?"

"It's a woman! And a man. They're walking away. Call out, don't lose them!"

We ran towards them for our lives. They did not appear startled at the raving idiots running out of the dark towards them.

"Are we near Sevenoaks?"

"About two miles."

"Still two miles!" we groaned.

"Would you like a lift?"

Would we like a lift! On the way to the station they told us they had not intended coming out but had just bought a new car and thought they would try it out.

"We like this wood," said the man.

We kept silent on that topic, but reckoned we had met our guardian angels that day.

Links and contacts

The Ramblers: *www.ramblers.org.uk*. Phone 020 7339 8500.

Open Spaces Society: *www.oss.org.uk*. Phone 01491 573535.

Long Distance Walkers Association: *www.ldwa.org.uk*.

British Walking Federation (IVV): *www.bwf-ivv.org.uk*.

Geoff's Jaunts (c/o Roger Kemp): *rogerjdkemp@yahoo.co.uk*. Phone 020 8350 1922.

National Railway Museum: *www.nrm.org.uk*. Phone 0844 815 3139.

Further reading

An Unrepentant Englishman – the life of S.P.B.Mais. Maisie Robson, The King's England Press, 2005. ISBN 978 1 872438 17 7.

Away for the day – the railway excursion in Britain, 1830 to the present day. Arthur and Elizabeth Jordan, Silver Link Publishing, 1991. ISBN 978 0 947971 63 2.

Walkers (a study of remarkable walkers of the past). Miles Jebb, Constable, 1986. ISBN 978 0 094674 30 1.

If you cannot obtain any of these books in a bookshop or from the publisher, try your local library, or:

Amazon: *www.amazon.co.uk*

AbeBooks: *www.abebooks.co.uk*

or other online booksellers.

The Ramblers. A Wikipedia article providing information about the origins and history of The Ramblers, formerly known as the Ramblers' Association, can be found at:
http://en.wikipedia.org/wiki/Ramblers.

Other publications by Colin Saunders

The Capital Ring
Aurum Press, 6th edition, 2014
ISBN 978 1 78131 337 4

The London Loop
with David Sharp, Aurum Press, 4th edition, 2012
ISBN 978 1 84513 787 8

The North Downs Way
Aurum Press, 2nd edition, 2013
ISBN 978 1 78131 061 8

London – the definitive walking guide
Cicerone Press, 2002
ISBN 978 1 85284 339 7

Walking in the High Tatras
with Renáta Nárožná, Cicerone Press, 3rd edition, 2012
ISBN 978 1 85284 682 4

Navigation and Leadership – a manual for walkers
Ramblers' Association, 1994
ISBN 978 0 90061 383 8

The Vanguard Way (North-South)
Vanguards Rambling Club, 5th edition, 2014
Online only at *www.vanguardway.org.uk*

The Vanguard Way (South-North)
Vanguards Rambling Club, 1st edition, 2011
Online only at *www.vanguardway.org.uk*

The Waymark Story
Footline Press, 2nd edition, 2013
Online only at *www.colinsaunders.org.uk*

The Strollerthon Story
In preparation

For more information please visit *www.colinsaunders.org.uk*.

The Berwick Inn at Berwick Station in East Sussex – better known in the heyday of the ramblers' excursions as the Fullers Arms.